Running Within

A Guide to Mastering the Body–Mind–Spirit Connection for Ultimate Training and Racing

Jerry Lynch, PhD

Warren A. Scott, MD

Human Kinetics

Library of Congress Cataloging-in-Publication Data

Lynch, Jerry, 1942–
    Running Within : a guide to mastering the body–mind–spirit connection for ultimate training and racing / Jerry Lynch, Warren A. Scott
        p.   cm.
    Includes bibliographical references and index.
    ISBN 0-88011-832-6
    1. Running—Psychological aspects. 2. Running—Training.
    I. Scott, Warren A. II. Title.
    GV1061.8.P75L856   1999
    796.42—dc21   99-11547
                                                                                  CIP

ISBN: 0-88011-832-6

Developmental Editor: Julie Rhoda; **Assistant Editor:** Sandra Merz Bott; **Copyeditor:** Jacqueline Blakley; **Proofreader:** Myla Smith; **Indexer:** Betty Frizzell; **Graphic Designer:** Nancy Rasmus; **Graphic Artist:** Kim Maxey; **Photo Editor:** Amy Outland; **Cover Designer:** Jack Davis; **Photographer (cover):** Tim De Frisco; **Photographer (interior):** Tom Roberts unless otherwise noted; **Printer:** United Graphics

Printed in the United States of America   10   9   8

Human Kinetics
Web site: www.HumanKinetics.com

United States: Human Kinetics, P.O. Box 5076, Champaign, IL 61825-5076
800-747-4457
e-mail: humank@hkusa.com

Canada: Human Kinetics, 475 Devonshire Road, Unit 100, Windsor, ON N8Y 2L5
800-465-7301 (in Canada only)
e-mail: orders@hkcanada.com

Europe: Human Kinetics, 107 Bradford Road, Stanningley
Leeds LS28 6AT, United Kingdom
+44 (0) 113 255 5665
e-mail: hk@hkeurope.com

Australia: Human Kinetics, 57A Price Avenue, Lower Mitcham, South Australia 5062
08 8277 1555
e-mail: liaw@hkaustralia.com

New Zealand: Human Kinetics, Division of Sports Distributors NZ Ltd.
P.O. Box 300 226 Albany, North Shore City, Auckland
0064 9 448 1207
e-mail: info@humankinetics.co.nz

To the late Steve Prefontaine,
who embraced his running as the essence of life itself.

Contents

Acknowledgments vi

Introduction *Outward Bound, Inward Bound* vii

Part I **Building Your Body–Mind–
Spirit Foundation** 1

Chapter 1 *Guiding Your Progress With Goals* 3

Chapter 2 *Relaxing to Excel* 15

Chapter 3 *Developing Positive Pictures* 29

Chapter 4 *Affirming Your Greatness* 39

Part II **Restructuring Attitudes for
True Success** 49

Chapter 5 *Exhibiting the Warrior Within* 51

Chapter 6 *Becoming Courageous on the Run* 61

Chapter 7 *Competing Is a Partnership* 71

Chapter 8 *Winning as a Journey* 77

Part III	Performing With Intent	85
Chapter 9	*Preparing for Race Day*	87
Chapter 10	*Examining and Transcending Limits*	101
Chapter 11	*Running in the Eye of a Hurricane*	109
Part IV	Hurdling Obstacles From Within	119
Chapter 12	*Flowing With Fatigue*	121
Chapter 13	*Gaining Without Straining*	129
Chapter 14	*Embracing Your Injury*	145
Chapter 15	*Reversing the Aging Process*	157
Part V	Running Beyond	165
Chapter 16	*Training for Mastery*	167
Chapter 17	*Experiencing the Mystical*	175
Chapter 18	*Dancing the Dance*	183
Epilogue	*Bonding With Kindred Spirits*	189
Index		192
About the Authors		198

Acknowledgments

Many thanks to Ted Miller for being the essential visionary for this project; to Julie Rhoda for her generosity, support, and acumen as an editor; to Marydell Forbes for her publicity savvy; and to all others at Human Kinetics for nurturing this book.

Outward Bound, Inward Bound

T hanks to the delicious victory by Frank Shorter in the 1972 Olympic marathon, distance running became a thriving, booming phenomenon in the 1970s. It grew at an epidemic rate as legions took to the streets, trails, and tracks, wanting to be part of the fitness mania. In 1979, membership in the Road Runners Club of America (RRCA) burgeoned to an astounding 45,000 enthusiasts. Races like the Peachtree 10K processed 20,000 applications. It seemed as though the country was in perpetual motion, obsessed with a newly discovered passion. Zealous runners would log 80-plus miles per week, working out twice a day every day. Moderation was anathema as *more is better* became the mantra for millions in motion.

In my early running days, I (Jerry) also was intent on logging 100 or more miles per week as if my self-worth as an athlete were measured by this century milestone. On one particular Saturday evening, I had just returned from a social engagement when it occurred to me at 11:20 P.M. that I had accumulated only 95 miles for the week—which was about to end in 40 minutes. In Clark Kent fashion, I jumped into my racing gear, went out the door, and cruised a 5-mile loop before the clock struck 12:00. I went to my training book and wrote in the big 1-0-0.

Those were the days when once you began a run, to stop along the way was to cancel the legitimacy of the experience; when a stoplight turned red, you might have to run in place until the light changed to green. This was the original definition of "wait" training, since few runners ever considered pumping iron back then. Stopping was never a consideration; the run wouldn't count. It was a time of speed, personal records (PRs), pulse rates, laps, miles, carboloading, and forcing the body on the road to unbalanced, compulsive, often out-of-control athletic pursuits.

Today, we understand better than ever the value of rest and time off; it's wise to give your body the opportunity to recoup after pushing the unlimited boundaries of your potential. Back in the early 1980s, it was common to go for a 20-mile run the day after a race, simply because you were afraid to rest and miss that Sunday long slow distance (LSD) workout.

Today, as we head into the third millennium, distance running has matured and is experiencing a second wind, a magical boom characterized by increased participation and renewed enthusiasm to compete and do well. However, for most of us the sport is considerably less formal and more mainstream, with a new maturity. We are still challenged by the outward expression of our running—racing and pushing ourselves to the edge—yet the challenge is also inward in the sense that we are our own opponents and our rewards are intensely personal. Victory is experienced by simply facing up to the challenge, and our external successes reflect our inner victories over fear, ego, self-doubt, frustration, fatigue, and other inner demons. Our running is multidimensional, melding overall mind and body wellness with mental and physical performance. Many of us view running as a mechanism that can improve and enrich our lives; it may not lengthen it (although many now believe it does), but it certainly widens it.

Perhaps you've noticed that running today is also more community based and socially oriented than it was in the 1970s and 1980s. More individuals than ever are running marathons, and marathons are also slower than ever. Families use the sport as a way to be together recreationally; for example, there are "Kids K" and "Diaper Dash" events that enable everyone to participate. Notice how at many races we compete not so much against each other, but more to *seek together* (the Latin meaning for the word *compete*) our outer boundaries of potential, where we find that our personal pace—when we are running beside others—can stretch comfortably to the next level.

As a group, we runners seem to be more sophisticated than ever in our use of new physiological and psychological findings; we are a wiser group, more open to learning about the inward journey and the body–mind–spirit connection provided by running. If you talk to other runners, you will find out that this is so. Many of you are interested in running as a means of learning more about who you are and what you are made of, particularly when your realities shrink to a dime at mile 22 of a marathon and you are called upon to dig deep to see what you have left. Running the roads, you begin to come across newer roads, the roads to self-discovery. The race itself becomes a road to spiritual awareness as you explore the meaning of all aspects of life and focus on your problems, concerns, joys, and fortunes. This exploratory experience not only creates the opportunity to become a better runner, but also to grow as a person.

Running has become a means of experiencing a personal potential greater than physical development. Your running workouts take you inward, away from outcomes and results, as you begin to test your limits, experience inner changes, identify your personal rhythms, and work out to your own inner beat. When you run in this way, you begin to experience more vitality, energy, flexibility, and spontaneity in all areas of life; you begin to recapture the deeper qualities of excitement, wonderment, and enthusiasm for greater fulfillment in the dynamic adventure of distance running.

Beyond Limits

Perhaps one of the most exciting and rewarding aspects of your running life is the potential to go beyond your self-imposed limitations. You begin to realize that many of your limiting beliefs about what can or cannot be done are simply preconceived restrictions and attitudes taught to you by parents, teachers, friends, and others during your formative years, with no objective basis in reality. The most damaging of these beliefs is the notion that such restrictions can never be changed and must be accepted without question as blueprints for your future. We are reminded of the bumblebee, which, according to experts in the fields of aerodynamics and space engineering, should not be capable of flying. After studying its attributes for many days, the experts concluded that the bee is too fat, too round, too slow, and not strong enough to fly. Fortunately, this little aviator cannot read these findings.

As we ventured out into the seas of uncertainty and self-doubt as children, we began to hear similar limiting messages. Many of us who are starting to run once again in our 30s, 40s, 50s, and beyond are told by the experts that we are too old, too heavy, too slow, or have the wrong mix of slow- and fast-twitch muscle fibers to be good distance runners. What these experts fail to consider is the right stuff we do have: our spirit, our strong mental composure, and our attitudes that have no room for negative litanies like *I can't, impossible, never could be, no way,* and other roadblocks to self-expansion. Many great runners have seen their determination to achieve become even greater at the sound of such ludicrous phrases. You, too, can question such utterances, challenge yourself, and go beyond limiting beliefs.

Rather than accept these preconceptions, you can dream about being a good runner and ask yourself, *Why not?* With that question as a modus operandi for your training program, you will begin to experience incredible breakthroughs into territories that you once feared. Your beliefs about what is now possible will become quite expansive. With the loss of weight; the accumulation of many miles of good, consistent, physical training; and the incorporation of healthy competitive mind-sets discussed in this book, you will experience yourself as an ultimate runner pushing back the boundaries of your potential.

Because most of us rarely utilize our full physical capability, we probably can't imagine where our real limits reside. When you become excited about discovering your unlimited potential, you may want to share this personal discovery with your friends who share the dream of self-expansion and personal development through running.

To this end, we've written *Running Within* as a training guide that provides specific ways to strengthen your body–mind–spirit potential. We've written this book for all runners who wish to take their performance to the next level—novices just getting into running for general health and fitness, competitive athletes of all ages, and veteran runners looking to light their running fires. Unlike many of the peak-performance books on the market, *Running Within* uniquely presents the reciprocal relationship among the physiological, mental, and spiritual aspects of running performance, and how you can use specific mental exercises and attitudinal shifts in your daily training and racing to great advantage. We provide you with concrete, hands-on strategies and exercises to help you maximize your mental performance and push your physical self to new heights. The psychophysiological evidence presented within each chapter supports the prescriptions, suggestions, recommendations, tools, and strategies we've provided to help you become your very best.

The body–mind–spirit aspects of performance, always recognized as important, are now finally getting the attention they deserve. Most of us are beginning to realize that we're overeducated about the physical and technical aspects of performance and seriously lacking with regard to the mental components of sport. For the most part, we start out as participants for fitness purposes and progress to higher levels of performance and competition.

When we see what is possible to achieve in our sport, beyond where we are at the moment, we reach a crossroads and search for more to help us improve. As we now understand that the mind rules the body, the body will do what the mind says it should. How you talk to your body involves the process of consistent, well-directed mental training as offered in this book.

Professional and Olympic athletes are employing our services to help maximize their performances; many recreational and competitive runners are also following suit. While working with some of the finest elite runners in the United States, we asked what percentage of their performance on any given day is attributed to their level of mental fitness. Invariably they state that it is about 80 to 90 percent; being mentally prepared is crucial and cannot be overlooked if one wants to be a complete athlete. These athletes never fail to reinforce what we already believe—limits are illusions or barriers that we manufacture for our unconscious convenience. The greatness of the African runners, for example, may be attributable to the notion that they have no illusions about not being able to run any faster. They regard no pace as too fast. This explains, in part, the quadruple world-record performance years ago by Kenyan distance phenom Henry Rono. According to world-class runner Kenny Moore, Rono had no illusions to hold him back; he regarded no record as unbreakable.

Runners must not impose barriers or limits on what is possible. We can and will begin to transcend our limits and go beyond the confines of our anatomical structures when we learn how to tune in to the powers of the mind. It is important to understand that the mind cannot help you to overcome your real physical, genetically based limitations; it does, however, allow you to go beyond what you *think* are your limits. There's an incredible amount of room for growth, change, and development within your running potential; your mental capabilities; and your emotional, spiritual self.

The most outrageous example of going beyond "thinking limits" in track and field was the superperformance by long jumper Bob Beamon during the 1968 Olympics in Mexico City. His extraordinary jump of 29 feet $2\frac{1}{2}$ inches was a full 2 feet farther than the world record. Most track experts feel this feat would be equivalent to lowering the men's world record in the mile from 3:44 to 3:25 in one race. Marathoners would have to run the 26.2-mile distance under 2 hours, something that most top runners would say is inconceivable based on the current world record for men. Competitors in both of these events will probably someday reach those mind-blowing levels of performance. After all, prior to Roger Bannister's breaking of the 4-minute barrier in the mile, over 50 reputable medical journals throughout the world claimed that such speed by a human was not only impossible, but unthinkable. Once Bannister transcended that "limit," more than 45 athletes mimicked his performance over the next year and a half. We find it hard to believe that all of those runners magically became so fast within that short time frame. A more likely explanation is that once the mental limit was lifted, the runners could see it as possible. The illusion of the impossibility of running under 4 minutes was shattered. Today, we have witnessed the breaking of the 8-minute barrier for 2 miles—that is, 2 miles, back-to-back, both under 4 minutes. We obviously possess greater capabilities than we believe we have.

As you embark upon this exciting new journey of integrating the body, mind, and spirit, expect to see radical changes as you push back the barriers of what you once thought were your limits. You are about to use a greater range of your physical and mental resources and actually feel the difference. The inner powers that you will discover are not new; you have had them for quite some time, but simply failed to use them. We speak about this inner exploration from our perspective as athletes who have experienced the benefits personally, as well as professionals and authors who understand and write about the theory. If benefits are to be had, you must be willing to exercise the mind consistently and often as a complete body–mind–spirit runner. Although it may require only 10 minutes daily to train the mind, you must do so with the same enthusiasm and commitment you devote to your physical development. If you do, there is no doubt that you will become your very best, more than capable of unleashing energy in ways that will enable you to feel your own personal greatness. When you do, your body, mind, and spirit will merge—not only for running, but for all arenas of performance throughout life.

We have all devoted an enormous amount of energy to the development of muscle strength, proper diet, endurance, race strategy, and coordination for the purposes of improvement. As we begin to level out with our performance, the need to develop the mind becomes even more important. The major breakthroughs in all running distances will now be reserved for those who train the mind on a regular and consistent basis.

Your Journey's Map

You are a multidimensional athlete composed of body, mind, and spirit. Collectively, you are greater than the sum of all parts, an integrated ordinary human capable of multiple extraordinary things. As you skim the contents of this book, you'll begin to comprehend the numerous facets of your runner persona. You are relaxed, visual, vocal, warriorlike, competitive, courageous, and more; and all are you, in the creation and emergence of what we call the body–mind–spirit runner. The purpose of this book is to nurture this runner in you, and encourage and guide you on your journey. To help you prepare for the journey, we provide a map of how we plan to guide you along the way to exploring your potential.

We lay the foundation in part I by offering you a broader-than-traditional perspective with regard to motivators and goals. Before you begin on your journey of running within, you need to first understand your personal motivations and how to use goals as milestones on this journey. Our outlook on motivation will help you to break away from the traditional notion of what winning means to develop your own definition. We then help you translate what winning means to you into developing goals that will guide you toward your running fulfillment.

Also, we build upon the foundational groundwork to give you specific tools you'll need to become a complete body–mind–spirit runner. Techniques for relaxation, visualization, and affirmation will help you add a new mental dimension to your physical workouts and racing and serve as constant companions as you come into your own.

Part II offers alternative attitudes and mind-sets to help you face the external challenges of performance more easily, as well as compete with your opponents within.

In part III, you will learn how to use your newfound skills and mind-sets to become more racewise and to take the necessary steps to transcend limiting beliefs and become more intent with your racing performance.

As you advance along this journey, you will be confronted with various obstacles that can block your way. Part IV provides the psychological and philosophical strategies to help mitigate the power and strength of these familiar friends along the path—

fatigue, overtraining, injury, and aging—so that you may progress more easily and freely.

Finally, part V gives you permission to experience the wider, deeper aspects of your sport. Here you will witness the mystical and masterful connection between your running exertion and the subsequent changes within your mind and spirit. You will discover that your running is a divine dance between you, the natural environment, and your spirit; the sacred time to simply play for part of the day. So fasten your seat belts and enjoy the journey.

I

Building Your Body—Mind—Spirit Foundation

You're on the path to becoming a runner who balances body, mind, and spirit with your running endeavor. Here in part I, we teach you the skills for adding a new dimension to your workouts and racing foundation. The mind-sets presented here will enable you to empty your mind of all the limiting ideas you have inherited about your running performance. They will open your mind to new, refreshing attitudes that allow you to redefine the boundaries you have mistakenly placed on your running potential.

Ancient Chinese wisdom tells us that the journey of a thousand miles begins with a single step. On the long and wide journey of becoming your personal best in the sport of distance running, you must take that first step of attending to the fires of your passion, of discovering motivation and using goals as beacons in the distance to keep you on track. For most of us, the terms *motivation* and *goals* are quite familiar, yet often extrinsic or results-oriented. We will open our minds to break away from traditional thinking about these time-honored concepts to embrace a different, more dynamic paradigm that clearly validates and nurtures the intrinsic benefits of the notion of running within. For example, a traditional goal may be to complete a marathon, which, in turn, motivates you to train in preparation. The emphasis on achieving this goal is the driving force, and if achieved, you feel complete and successful; if not, you consider the attempt a failure. However, if we look at the goal (in this case, completing a marathon) as a lesson, or a light in the distance that keeps us on track to achieve an even greater goal (the lifestyle of a well-trained athlete) we experience a deeper, more substantial sense of achievement in our attempt to run a marathon.

In part I, we present you with ways to discover your motivators and translate these into meaningful goals that will allow you to enjoy the path taken to reach the goals as much as—if not more than—arriving at the goal itself (chapter 1). We then provide you with some important mental skills to build upon this base: relaxation (chapter 2), visualization (chapter 3), and positive affirmation (chapter 4). Used collectively, these skills will help you directly link your mental training and emotions to your physical performance.

Like a parachute, the mind works best when open. Open up to the possibilities along the road to becoming the best you can be by practicing these inner skills for 10 to 15 minutes every day that you physically work out. Practicing these skills on a consistent basis will assure you that they will work for you when you need them most—whether during tough workouts, while healing yourself during an injury, or during a prerace warm-up.

We also recommend that if you are maintaining a running logbook—and we strongly encourage you to do so—you should make a place for mental notations as well, right next to the physical data you record. The idea is to enrich your running by including, side by side, the mental, emotional, and spiritual happenings along with the physical. Writing these reflections reinforces the use of these mental skills and helps you to visit these reactions and feelings in the future and learn from them.

Guiding Your Progress With Goals

A talented runner visited his coach at home to talk about changes in his workout routine. While there, he picked up a delicate trophy made of crystal. The trophy slipped out of his hands and shattered into many pieces. The athlete, shaken by his carelessness, expressed deep regret for his action. The coach, always quick with his Zen wisdom, reassured the athlete that the treasure is not the trophy, but the experience he had in the process of winning it—the joy, pleasure, and fulfillment of striving each day.

A 60-year-old athlete we know had set a goal of running under 3 hours in a marathon. After numerous unsuccessful attempts, a friend asked why he persisted in what seemed to be a futile journey into the forest of frustration. The athlete quickly responded that the attainment of the goal was not his ultimate objective. The goal was his excuse to experience a full life of training at high levels, getting into great shape, eating healthy foods, and feeling terrific. The goal simply became the beacon that illuminated his journey toward fitness and wellness.

It's not that attaining a goal has no value in and of itself. We need goals as beacons to give us something to strive for, and we need both beacons that are near us (short-term goals) and beacons that are farther away (long-term goals). However, the process of arriving at that beacon, passing it, and looking for the next one is what causes our inner selves to flourish and grow. It's exciting to achieve your goals, but to do so for the sake of achievement alone may exclude you from experiencing the joy in the moment, separating you from the deeper essence of running. For example, I (Jerry) have run to the top of a mountain with the lone goal of getting to that summit; but I prefer to take the path that meanders through the wildflowers and dance with the deer and other natural phenomena around me as I am softly led to the pinnacle with little effort . . . same goal, different path. In the latter case, I enjoy the process much more than the arrival.

Once you make this shift in consciousness, you open yourself to endless opportunities to nurture your spirit and discover the real reasons you run. You also cease to measure your self-worth according to external outcomes and results, and thus nurture your self-esteem.

Motivation is the direct result of love for what you are doing, whether you love the recognition; the accomplishment; or simply

Photo © Ron Dahlquist

the motion, the flow, the effort. In this chapter, we help you
discover what it is you personally love about running and provide
ways to help you incorporate this love into your foundational
goalsetting. By discovering what started you running, we aim to
help you light, reignite, or keep the fires of motivation and
inspiration burning for as long as possible. Adopting this new
paradigm—to seek what the journey has to offer—reduces anxiety
and stress. This reduced stress, paradoxically, will help you
ultimately to achieve your goals.

What Motivates You?

Let's begin with any of you who may be new to the sport. Know that some struggle at the outset is normal. Most beginning distance runners start and stop an average of 13 times before becoming "runners." The initial phases of breaking into the running lifestyle are often filled with frustration, disillusionment, aches, and pains. To strengthen your fun, joy, and motivation with your beginning running routine, try a gentle program of alternating running with walking. Think about this approach as a moving meditation that enables you to work out aerobically while contemplating (in the walking phase) the soft, fluid motion of your exercise, your private rhythm, and thoughts about life. Do you have questions on your mind? Decisions to make? Problems to solve? Here is your opportunity to focus on these issues and gain perspective. The running segment gives you the chance for a more powerful, energetic, in-your-comfort-zone conditioning period. Together they represent a soft-hard, slow-fast, inner-outer dance that can keep your interest and motivation primed for quite awhile. In the long haul, alternating as a means of staying motivated is beneficial not just with running and walking, but with other activities as well—cycling, swimming, lifting weights, and so on.

Begin by allocating 45 minutes for your workout, and divide the time into 5-minute segments. Start out by walking 4 minutes and running 1 minute. Repeat this pattern for each of the nine segments within the 45-minute session. Depending on your level of fitness and rate of improvement, begin to increase the running by 1-minute segments and decreasing the walk time equally; the walk–run ratio looks like this: 4 to 1, 3 to 2, 2 to 3, 1 to 4. In the last ratio, you are running a full 36 minutes.

Start with two sessions per week for the first two to three weeks. You may cross-train on two other days per week initially. If all seems well, add a third walk–run session, starting out short and easy and then building on the running time. Continue with three walk–run sessions per week (and two to three cross-training sessions per week) for one to two months. Take your time with the progression. If you desire to add a fourth running day, repeat the original pattern of breaking the fourth day into nine 5-minute segments. If you allow one to two months for adaptation to occur, you can then add a fifth and sixth running day. Be prepared to back up and skip some days to balance the stress-versus-rest equation.

Try substituting cross-training days for running days as you are progressing. The walking interval provides a nice rest period for your body. Expand this notion of daily minute segments to weekly segments. Work up to running four days and walking one day. This gives your body a full two days to recover and prevents burnout and injury (from overtraining). Try this or some variation of it, and notice how high your motivation and interest soar.

By taking a more moderate approach, you increase the likelihood of experiencing many of the wonderful benefits of your program—weight loss, a more relaxed daily existence, and increased amounts of endorphins (the body's own opiates that result in the feeling of a "runner's high") released in your brain. These added benefits can motivate you to continue the program.

Where Are You Going?

Now that you are focused on exploring the joy of the process of attaining your goals, it's time to look more closely at what goals you set out for yourself on the horizon. Are they close enough that you can see their glow? Or are they too far away to even be seen? Perhaps they are lined up like stepping stones, one leading to the other. The following guidelines will help you formulate goals that challenge your body, mind, and spirit.

Evaluate Your Abilities

It is crucial to be honest in evaluating your abilities as an athlete. You want to establish *realistic* goals to avoid the crushing feelings of failure, frustration, and disappointment. Yet you don't want to sell yourself short in the process. There is often a wide gap between your real limits and what you believe to be your limits. You must examine what you think are your limits and go beyond them.

In assessing your limits, establish realistic but challenging short-term goals. Since you are likely to achieve these goals frequently, you will reinforce the psychological message that you are a winner and you can accomplish your goals. This will ignite courage, confidence, motivation, and commitment for future directions.

Be sure these goals are in concert with your lifestyle. Working 60 hours per week would certainly interfere with running nationally competitive times, regardless of your physical attributes. On the other hand, perhaps you have 20 hours a week to devote to training, yet the physical components are in short supply. In any event, talk to a runner friend, spouse, or coach—someone who can help you to assess your abilities more objectively. Based on your workouts and short race performances, you may be surprised to know that you are underestimating your abilities or overestimating the difficulty of the event.

At a prerace seminar, a participant asked me (Jerry) if his goal for the marathon was realistic. He wanted to run a 2:55, having already completed a 2:59:17. After reviewing his training log and 10K times, I felt he was being a bit conservative; four weeks prior to our conversation, he had run a 35:31 10K. (Most race prediction charts indicate that such a time translates into a 2:47 marathon.)

You've probably heard the phrase *What you can conceive you can achieve.* If you feel that something you want is possible, go for it, and in time you will reach it. Of course, the evidence must indicate that it is possible. I decided to explore this with him. I asked him, "How about 2:35?"

"No way!" he exclaimed.

"Well, then 2:40?"

"Not quite yet," he hesitantly replied. (This hesitation is a cue that a realistic goal is being approached.) I then suggested a 2:45, which drew a quick "Maybe." He seemed ready to explore a new horizon. When I suggested a 2:48, he said, "Under perfect conditions, I could probably do that." He pointed out his fear of setting that up as a goal, and I suggested that he instead choose a range within which success would be realized.

He promised to visualize the possibility of a 2:46 to 2:55 for the upcoming marathon. He needed to affirm this possibility so that if he was on a 2:48 pace at mile 18, he wouldn't panic—it was within the range. If he was on a 2:55 pace, that would also be acceptable. Three weeks after the race, I received a postcard. All it said was, "Incredible—2:47:36—thanks." (Note that we'll discuss visualization and affirmation techniques in chapters 3 and 4, respectively.)

You can try this process yourself. Choose a time that is about 7 percent faster than what you know you can run at this point. That new time will appear unreasonable, so start counting back as I did above. The very moment you can say *I can see that happening* or *It's possible,* stop—this is your new realistic range. Be sure to see it as a *range* that allows for the unexpected happening. A 2:30 marathoner, for example, will have a range of 2:20:50 to 2:30; I'll bet that a 2:27:34 sounds realistic to him. Mentally gear yourself for that eventuality. If you fail to reach the new goal right away, don't despair. Patience and persistence will enable you to arrive as long as the training process is fulfilling and fun.

Incorporate Other Life Objectives

Perhaps you are a runner and an amateur photographer, and your husband loves to travel. You have two children and wish to spend quality time with them. Why not plan a family trip to a fun race and take some good photos of the points of interest? Such combining of goals into one project can bring a sense of joy and fulfillment to all involved. Altruistically or not, the family will support your efforts all the way. The possibilities are limitless. How about the London Marathon?

Share Your Goal

Aside from family support, try to get someone of equal ability to share your goal. With mutual objectives, you can be an endless source of encouragement and inspiration for each other; you can spur one another on when discouragement sets in. Your workouts together will become more enjoyable, particularly those that require hard-track efforts or long, lonely distance sojourns. Improvement will be rapid as each of you will invariably alternate pushing each other to run a bit faster than planned. Such an arrangement plays into your competitive nature and helps to bring out your best.

Be Patient and Persistent

With patience and persistence, your goals will be realized, and you'll embrace the challenge to body, mind, and spirit with each step you take toward this goal. Although delay of gratification is difficult to contend with, you will be rewarded for your persistence if you get up just one more time than you fall. A steam engine's effort to pull 100 cars at a water temperature of 211 degrees is futile. Yet one more measly degree of heat to reach the boiling point will enable that same engine to barrel up and over a mountain pass lugging a century of coal cars behind it. What if it quit after reaching the 211 degrees? Sometimes all you need for a major breakthrough in your performance is "one more degree" of persistence.

Improvement through goalsetting is also a process of trial and error; such a process is time consuming and demands patience and persistence. Two steps forward and one back will still eventually get you to your destination. Being impatient, however, can actually interfere with goal attainment. To be impatient is to create stress that directly inhibits the natural fluidity of your muscles, thus preventing you from performing optimally. This happened with an elite athlete at a major West Coast university. He wanted to run 27:50 for 10K on the track—*now!* He raced often—too often, perhaps—only to become terribly frustrated and disappointed, never being able to do better than 28:03. He impatiently pushed harder in his workouts in order to get better, until finally, tired of waiting and tired of training, he decided two weeks before the NCAA championships to run under 28 minutes in a regional track meet. The pressure, tension, and stress mounted and wreaked havoc with his body until, three days before the race, he severely injured his right Achilles tendon. Relieved, strangely, from the pressure he had created, he decided to shelve his efforts and back off his obsession.

He struggled to understand his dilemma. He began to see how his impatience and unwillingness to delay gratification contributed to his stress, which ultimately caused tension in his musculoskeletal system, setting the stage for injury. Following a four-week layoff, he came back rejuvenated with a new perspective on the matter. Within three weeks, without self-induced pressure, he clocked a magnificent 27:46. A goal is like the elusive butterfly—you can chase one for hours and come up empty-handed. But lie down in the field and be patient, and one will probably land on your nose.

Embrace Your Setbacks

Since the goalsetting process is one of trial and error, you must remember that setbacks are to be expected; they are a natural consequence of taking a risk and trying to improve. They are

temporary, however, and are actually opportunities to learn and reevaluate your situation. With new data from the setback—*I went out too fast; I surged too early; I overtrained and ran tired*—you can reestablish new goals and proceed accordingly with the updated information.

Many athletes have run a series of progressively slower races prior to a major personal best. Olympic gold medalist Joan Benoit Samuelson, before her 1983 Boston Marathon victory, ran a series of marathons ranging from 2:30 to 2:37, each one slower than the previous attempt. This would discourage the best of us—but not Joan. Learning from each experience, she proceeded according to the data, running a splendid world-record performance that year at Boston in 2:22:43. By the way, her near-suicidal pace (5:27 per mile) would have won every men's Olympic marathon up to 1960.

Visualize Your Goals

One of the strongest support systems you have is your mind's eye. Clearly see yourself reaching your goal, and experience in your mind how that would feel. The clearer your imagery and picture of achievement, the easier it is to accomplish the task. As we know it, the central nervous system does not distinguish between real and imagined events; your body will follow the visualized images as if they were real. We have seen athletes hooked up to an electromyograph machine (a device that measures muscle response and activity) and, in a deeply relaxed state, told to visualize running up and down a hill. With the athletes resting in a "sleep state" on a table, the graph recorded movement of those muscles necessary for climbing and descending hills; they responded simply to the images alone. Apply the concept of visual imagery to your goals, and you will have strong support in your attainment of those objectives. Remember—what you see is what you get. Try this while in a deeply relaxed state of mind:

> Set a running goal that will create a joyful process.
>
> Feel the joy, excitement, and fun that accompanies this journey.
>
> Imagine yourself growing and improving as an athlete.
>
> Feel exhilarated as you live the lifestyle of a well-trained runner.
>
> Remind yourself that the goal is the beacon, guiding you to fulfillment.
>
> Imagine the goal being accomplished, and search for another that will help you continue the journey.

Chapter 3 will give you the skills you need to incorporate visualization into your training and racing.

Affirm Your Goals

Affirmations are short, concise imagery phrases that, when repeated often enough, create the clarity and confidence you need to reach your goals. A few examples follow.

Lean and trim, I run to win.
Silky, smooth, and swift, I run to get a lift.
Every day, in every way, I excel and run well.
The arrival is nice, but the journey is best.
Goals are beacons that keep me on track.
I love the journey as much as the destination.

The body is extremely suggestible and receptive to such images. Create your own self-suggestions. In a relaxed state of mind, repeat the phrase over and over. The statement should reflect your beliefs about yourself (or what you will become in the future). State it as if it were already true. Choose only those ideas that are possible for you, even if they haven't been realized.

Many runners ask, *Is it better to announce my goals, or should I keep them secret?* We answer, whatever makes you feel most comfortable. Some runners feel anxious and pressured once their goal is publicized, and such stress will likely interfere with their performances. Once announced, your goals may be subject to the scrutiny of your peers; there will be the barrage of questions when you return from the race: *What was your time? Did you place?* I (Jerry) have made the mistake of telling the world of my plans to run a PR at a national championship 10K race. With great expectations, and even greater pressure, I registered my first DNF (did not finish), dropping out at mile 4—totally exhausted, tight, and feeling like a beached whale. I didn't want to come home again and face those questions. The thought of running a race in the future looked dismal at best. I needed five months away from competition. Some friends suggested that I jump back into it; but honestly, my mind would not permit it.

On the other hand, goal pronouncement can actually be helpful. If used wisely, it can strengthen your commitment and motivation, and gives those who know your intentions a chance to rally around you and support your efforts. You must ultimately decide when it's good to let the secret out.

The basic notion of running within with regard to goals is to celebrate both the process created by setting such objectives and the natural by-product of such joy, the actual attainment of your goals. Chapter 2 will provide you with more specific tools and exercises to help you strengthen and apply these concepts.

chapter 2

Relaxing to Excel

It was the morning after the Boston Marathon, and the *Boston Globe*'s headline spoke about the narrow victory of Bill Rodgers over the fast-closing Dick Beardsley. Inching out his close nemesis in one of the race's most exciting finishes of all time, "Boston Billy" claimed that with less than 100 meters to go, he could see in his mind's eye his own version of the headline if he lost to Beardsley. That frightening thought pushed the adrenaline throughout his body, ultimately propelling him to victory. Rodgers claimed that his fear of failure at that moment was an important motivational factor that led to the victorious outcome of the race.

Reading this account might lead you to believe that high anxiety is the key to running your best; and in Bill's 8- to 10-second burst in this race, it may have been. Yet had he felt this anxious, tense, and stressed throughout the entire event, he might have withered miles before the Newton Hills.

Years ago, I (Jerry) believed that I couldn't be too relaxed for an event, and decided to test my hypothesis to the extreme. Prior to an important 20K race, I engaged my body in a wonderfully relaxing yoga session. After two hours of various stretching postures, I found myself extremely relaxed, and believed I was ready to race. I was so relaxed that I barely made it to the race before the start! I even forgot my racing shoes at home. Fifteen minutes into the event, I noticed how familiar competitors, the ones I normally beat, were floating past me—yet I didn't care, because I was totally out of it. After another 10 minutes, my adrenaline began to kick in; I came alive, surged, and began to reel in most of those who had previously passed me. However, I never quite came into my own, and finished out of the top 10 in a race I expected to win because I started to come alive too late. I was *too* relaxed.

This was an important lesson in moderation for me: there is a delicate balance between being relaxed and comfortably aroused. This balance is something that we all become sensitive to with experience, and we must develop that balance in order to reach our full potential as runners. If you monitor a few of your races, you will begin to notice your personal relaxed state that typically precedes your better performances. Most of us run better when we achieve this delicate balance. Once you establish what your personal level of optimal relaxation is, you can use the principles in this chapter to control your optimal desired state of arousal and relaxation prior to a race. Regardless of your personal level of arousal, optimal performances on any given day relate directly to your ability to stay away from those overly excitable levels that create wasted nervous energy and detract from your ability to do your best.

Neurophysiology of Stress and Relaxation

Let's take a look at the basics of neurophysiology to better understand the way the mind and body optimally interact. The brain can be divided into three main parts: the brain stem and spinal cord, the limbic system, and the cerebral cortex. The overall functioning of the brain requires a blending of these three parts.

The brain stem operates at the unconscious level, producing electrical impulses that control basic bodily functions such as breathing and heart rate. The limbic system is responsible for behavioral and emotional reactions, and operates at both the conscious and unconscious levels. The wakefulness centers of the brain are situated here. The limbic system controls survival instincts such as eating, sleeping, bowel and bladder function, and sexual behavior. The limbic brain is our automatic, reflexive, primitive, emotional, behavioral brain.

In contrast, the cerebral cortex is our higher-consciousness, thinking brain responsible for information storage, memory, abstract thought, sensory, and motor functioning. A finely tuned running style is controlled by our cerebral cortex. It is here that we can tell ourselves to run tall, long, smooth strides, and to swing arms freely with hands and fingers slightly clenched. This information is relayed through the limbic system, which, in turn, relays it to the spinal cord, and eventually to the arms and legs. Sounds simple enough—yet this relay via the limbic system is quite tricky.

You see, any negative, stressful, confusing thought patterns will disrupt the sequence of brain commands that tell you to relax by detouring the neural pathways through the limbic system. Limbic system arousal is an important part of readiness for sports or activities, but intense limbic stimulation produces a paradoxical state that increases tension. You will try to relax, but you will find the distress level too high to overcome. Relax! You can learn how to master control of the limbic system during your runs. This powerful yet primitive area of the brain ultimately governs the higher cortical functions. Try this experiment: use your conscious cortical brain functions to force yourself to stop breathing. Take a deep breath. Hold it. Go! Now count to yourself: one, two, three, four, five. For most of us, the will to stop breathing will be challenged within 60 seconds by a far greater "will." Reflexive centers in the limbic system and brain stem start discharging messages that supersede the higher cortex, forcing you to breathe again.

Now, imagine that you are sitting in your living room, quietly relaxing in your favorite easy chair. Your belly is full and your bones are weary. You're reading the paper, and you begin to feel tired. Your eyes begin to open and close, coupled with slower breathing patterns and reduced heartbeats. Then—kaboom! Your child pops a balloon right over your head and scares the living daylights out of you. Your heart begins to pound, your respiration increases, your palms become sweaty, and you have a lump in your throat. About 10 minutes later, you settle down to normal.

Now, sit in your easy chair and think about making your heart speed up, as it did when the balloon popped. Try to will your heart to speed up. Can you do it as easily as the balloon did? I hope you can see how our level of control over ourselves changes under different circumstances. For our purposes in cultivating ourselves as inner runners, we want to teach you how to better read your level of arousal (on an excited-versus-relaxed continuum) and how to promote cortical function over limbic function to help you relax.

About 17 years ago, I (Warren) found myself running with a friend who happened to be a psychologist for the University of Alabama Medical School. I was relating some distressful news, and within seconds felt my ankle give way, precipitated by landing on an acorn. My friend suggested that the stressful discussion upset my runner's balance and led to the stumble. Immediately following the sprain I reflected, *What was I thinking at the instant of the twist?* Since then, every running mishap I've had has been preceded by negative emotions such as anger, sadness, anxiety, or fear. The physiological analysis of this situation illustrates the limbic–cortical balance. Negative emotions in

the limbic system can disrupt the neurologic pathways between the cerebral cortex and the leg muscles. This millisecond detour is just enough time to create a misstep. Think about those times when you got injured on a run; how often did the accident occur when you were stressed, anxious, or tense? We believe you will find that there is a strict direct correlation between injury and stress (see chapter 14, p. 152).

Relaxing for Optimal Performance

Edwin Moses, Peter Snell, Abebe Bikila, Henry Rono, Billy Mills, Tosheiko Seko, Bob Kennedy, Joan Benoit Samuelson, Grete Waitz, Anne Marie Lauck, and other great runners over the years would all agree that they share one quality: the ability to relax and self-regulate their levels of prerace arousal. This same ability—the ability to relax the mind and body—is the most widely ignored aspect of training programs for elite and recreational runners alike, yet also happens to be the most crucial for performance. Australian runner Rob de Castella, one of the world's greatest marathoners ever, considered his ability to settle down and physically and mentally relax before a race to be one of his greatest strengths, and recommended that every athlete should seek such ability. This is not to say, however, that certain circumstances in his racing didn't call for greater arousal. Overall, a relaxed, calm nature was crucial to his success over the long run. Being calm enables one to focus energy when and where it is needed. Also, it helps the musculoskeletal system to remain fluid for greater, more efficient striding throughout the run. In a phrase, we need to *relax for the max*imum performance.

This notion of relaxation as a prerequisite to running success has been reinforced in our work with elite distance runners who compete in races ranging from the 1500-meter to the marathon. They unanimously agree that the secret key to smoother, faster, championship performance is to focus on relaxation and remain calm before and during the event. You can experiment with the techniques in the next section before and during races to learn which methods bring about this calm for you.

Relaxed running leads to peak performance. To remain relaxed, we must use our cerebral cortex and sensory and motor areas of our brains, and keep the limbic system quiet. Intense feelings and negative thoughts can stimulate the limbic centers and increase your baseline level of tension and anxiety. This can precipitate a circular pattern in which feelings of anxiety (butterflies in your stomach, a lump in your throat, sweaty palms, increased breathing and heart rates) can cause emotional panic—which, in turn, stimulates those parts of the brain that further increase the respiratory and heart rates. This can multiply and eventually cause a full-blown panic attack. This happened in 1988 to an

American Olympic athlete in Korea, who jumped off a bridge during such an episode and remains permanently injured. For most of us, we may get a feeling that we are "losing it" before or during a race.

Years ago, the head track coach at San Jose State, Bud Winter, espoused the benefits of running relaxed in his classic book *Relax and Win.* He developed the 90 percent law, claiming that when an athlete gives 100 percent, she gets tense and, paradoxically, performs at lower levels than if she exerted a 90 percent effort. You can see the 90 percent law in action if you watch a distance race of elite athletes. They are going fast—their splits tell the tale—yet they look smooth and effortless, almost as if they are out for a leisurely run. You can achieve this relaxed running, too, by focusing on running in control and on the mechanics of arm swing or foot plant, and maintaining a certain rhythm and pace.

National 5000-meter champion Ceci St. Geme mentioned that she felt very relaxed during her national-championship perfor-mance, and the race seemed so effortless, so easy. To remain calm during the race, Ceci focused her attention on the process of the race, such as tactics, form, stride, and posture, rather than poten-tial outcomes and results. By taking her mind away from what might eventually happen (the outcome) she reduced her anxiety associated with trying to control what can't be controlled—the results. Also, she practiced the ancient wisdom of *soft is strong;* the martial art of aikido teaches that the less resistance, force, and effort you create, the more efficient and effective you become. This same principle can be applied to running, as physiologically it helps to conserve energy and direct it in a positive, useful direction. Therefore, if you want to run faster, focus on running smarter.

You can experience the difference for yourself: first, do three push-ups with your arms tensed, then do three more with your arms firm but relaxed. Notice how the second set was much easier. Similarly, the implication for running hills is simple but powerful: relax to create the max. Most runners tend to apply more power and run the hills harder. However, *harder* in some runners' minds translates to tenser bodies. Instead, try relaxing your shoulders, arms, and face as you glide up the trail; notice the difference. There's no need to get tough to run hills. You need power, but it is a fluid, controlled, relaxed power rather than tense power. Inefficient movement leads to premature fatigue, loss of running economy, and, consequently, suboptimal performances. Focus on relaxing as you run your hills: imagine helium balloons attached to your shoulders, lifting you as you proceed to run up the hill like a tireless deer. Repeat the words *Relax, relax, relax . . . soft is strong.*

Understanding the following physiological responses to relaxation will encourage you to practice being calm prior to any workout or race. Remind yourself often of the rewards that are available to you with regular, consistent relaxation practice.

• Relaxed muscles are more fluid and contribute to greater coordination, strength, and endurance.

• Relaxed bodies react more quickly. Anxiety, fear, and tension inhibit your reaction time. Relaxed runners, on the other hand, react to challenging, difficult race conditions more quickly and make crisp decisions when confronted with unexpected obstacles and changes.

• Relaxed bodies burn less energy by keeping inappropriate and useless stress in check. As a result, fatigue is reduced. Tension contracts the blood vessels, inhibiting the flow of blood to the muscles and causing fatigue; relaxation reverses this process.

• Relaxation lowers blood lactate (lactic acid). Research shows that this lactate, the accumulation of which inhibits performance, decreases in calm athletes or is less in calm athletes than it is in tense athletes.

• Both concentration and the ability to focus improve when you are relaxed, positively affecting your confidence. Increased confidence in your ability to run improves your self-image, making success more likely.

Ways to Relax

There is absolutely no one right way to relax; some methods work for some and not for others. You may even have a unique method that works best for you. For example, you may have a relaxing prerace routine, or a song you like to listen to. Perhaps you like to take a nap, chill out before a workout, or think of a getaway place before a race; you may like being alone or being around certain people to relax. Harry Groves, head track and cross-country coach at Penn State University, has a special way of his own. He sees the bright side of everything, so it's relaxing just to be around him. He seems to pass this attitude on to his squad, creating an ideal, relaxed environment for performance. At a recent Penn Relays championship, a team member approached Coach Groves and expressed concern about how his father would feel if he didn't run a good race. Groves quietly replied, "Look, if you run the race of your life, your father will definitely love you. But if you don't run well, your father will still love you, and so will I. Now, get your butt out there and have a great time."

The young man did just that, and in the process brought home a wonderful treat. With the pressure off, he ran the most relaxed race of his life for a stunning win while setting a school and meet record. Many techniques like Harry's are available that can help you to experience such states of relaxation. Experiment and find one that works for you.

Breathwatching

Most of us take very shallow breaths through our mouths with considerable amounts of usable oxygen lost in the process of repeated exhalation. A more natural, effective method of respiration is to breathe through the nostrils and allow the breath to penetrate and circulate throughout the entire body, from your head down to your toes. Get into the habit of practicing this form of meditation for 5 minutes followed by visualization for 10 minutes (see chapter 3) prior to every workout or race. It is a great, simple technique that you can master in a short period of time. This relaxation approach will help you to see fitness, exercise, and running as an internal martial art, a new Zenlike way of body conditioning.

1. Sit comfortably in a chair, keeping your back naturally upright and planting your feet in front, with legs open naturally from your hips.
2. Close your eyes to reduce external stimulation.
3. Inhale very slowly through your nostrils, and with closed eyes "watch" the white cloud of air as it fills the lungs completely.

4.   Elongate the breath for a few seconds and "see" the clean air travel to all parts of the body down to your toes. Imagine this breath picking up your tensions and toxins.

5.   Slowly release the air through the nostrils, and notice the natural relaxation that occurs when the now-gray cloud filled with toxins, stress, and negativity exits as carbon dioxide. "See" this smoky deoxygenated cloud dissolve into thin air and disappear.

6.   At complete exhalation, once again suspend breathing for a second or two and imagine the wide-open emptiness of your lungs before you resume inhalation.

7.   Repeat this process 10 or more times. Gradually, feel your breathing spreading and penetrating outward into your arms and legs until the breath reaches the tips of your fingers and toes.

When you have become comfortable with this technique sitting down, you can begin to practice it in a standing position, and eventually use it in your workout routine, warm-up, and race. Once you have mastered this state, you can begin to introduce the skills of visualization and affirmation recitation detailed in the following two chapters.

Deer, horses, and most other animals use their noses to breathe while running. Breathing through your nostrils and allowing the oxygen to filter through the entire body will help you gain quicker access to your relaxed self, where performance can be optimized. Once you begin to practice this on a consistent basis, you will grow more adept and find it to be quite natural. Start by taking it slow; get in the habit of using this technique in your warm-up mile, and maintain an easy pace that allows nose breathing. You will eventually, if not immediately, begin to empty the mind in a state of quiet meditation where you achieve what is called inner stillness. Ultimately, you will carry this over to your running, creating stillness in motion, where your body, mind, and spirit are in synchronicity.

Facewatching

During a workout or race, use the "let the meat hang on the bones" routine. It is commonly known that your facial muscles control most of the tension in the rest of the body. Simply relax your face and let the skin hang down on the face bones, and you will automatically create a looseness throughout the body. Soften your eyes, loosen your jaw, and relax your neck. Think of water—it's fluid and yielding, soft yet strong. Soften the hardness of your face, and notice how much more fluid your body becomes. Notice other runners in the race; they seem very serious with tight, tense faces. Smile, and you will relax all over and maybe even pass a few of the frowners.

Bodywatching

Follow these suggestions as you run, in conjunction with the breathwatching and facewatching, until you eventually develop the habit of running relaxed.

1. Keep your upper body perpendicular to the running surface. Pull your shoulders back slightly and push your buttocks forward.

2. Keep your hands softly closed as if you were holding onto delicate paper cylinders.

3. Stride smoothly. Try to avoid over- and understriding, as these waste incredible amounts of energy.

4. Relax the shoulders and carry arms low. Shoulders should remain loose, yet stable. Elbows can be firm, but not locked. The tip of your thumb should brush by your waist at the point where the top of a pocket would be.

5. Move faster by focusing on relaxation rather than on applying power.

Wordwatching

Be cognizant of the words you focus on while running, and choose positive, active words. Rather than saying *run hard,* say *run smart;* don't tell yourself to *push,* say *glide* and *float* in its place. Learn to use a cue word during your performance as a stimulus for the relaxed state. For example, on occasion, you may say the word *calm* or *relax* out loud, following each with four or five pronounced deep breaths. This will reinforce the connection between what your mind is saying to you and what your body is doing. As you say the cue word, feel the stillness spread throughout the body.

Relaxing the Senses

Try the following exercise prior to workouts and races in conjunction with relaxed breathwatching. Be sure to find a quiet place, free from distraction.

1. With eyes closed, breathe deeply five times.

2. Imagine a strong, radiant, yellow beam of sunlight entering the top of your head. See and feel the warm light permeate your skull, neck, and shoulders, moving out your arms to your fingertips, into your chest cavity, throughout your back muscles, down to your abdomen, into your legs and the tips of your toes. It continues to flow throughout your entire body, down to the very last cell, warming and relaxing the tissue.

3. Notice how this warm ray nourishes each molecule, creating enormous health, vibrancy, and energy. Feel yourself totally relaxed, full of strength and ready to run.

4. Imagine yourself out on your favorite course; you float across the course easily, effortlessly, dancing with the terrain beneath you. You are calm and relaxed, running like a champion.

Practice this exercise on a regular basis. Make it part of your routine prior to your workouts, and you will begin to self-regulate the impact of tension on every run. To assist in this regard, couple the visualization with affirmations (discussed in chapter 4) to reinforce the state of relaxation.

> I relax and achieve the max.
> When I relax my jaw, I get so much more.
> Let my skin hang on my bones.
> Smile to go the extra mile.
> Calm . . . relax . . . tranquil.

Relaxed Stimulation

As we mentioned in the beginning of the chapter, some of you might find yourselves too flat, uninspired, and in need of a high level of arousal—you are too relaxed and calm. The purpose of the following exercises is to help you self-regulate and increase your arousal level by stimulating the flow of adrenaline and creating a positive level of excitement. Being too calm and lethargic has as many drawbacks as being at the other end of the arousal continuum. The following exercises will help the body get revved; if you still feel "blah" and unenthused, consider not racing that day, or running the race as a workout or fun run.

Breath control. Clench your fists, tighten your jaw, and begin to take short, rapid, deep breaths. After 60 seconds, you will notice the body's tempo quickly elevating. Take more time if needed. Be careful not to hyperventilate.

Rapid focus. The object of this exercise is to stimulate the flow of information to the brain. Focus on an object, person, or place; quickly observe every possible detail. Rapidly change your attention to something else, then repeat the process. Your eyes and head should scan the environment as quickly as possible, focusing as you go.

Music manipulation. Just as you use music to create calm and tranquility, choose favorite tunes that energize. It's difficult to remain mellow with "up" music. Carry a cassette or CD player, or blast the sound from the car stereo. Come alive with the sound of music by manipulating the tempo and volume.

Prance or dance. Any form of rapid movement to include quick, sharp turns and fast steps will affect your energy level in a positive way. Three quick steps forward, turn left for seven rapid strides, turn right and briskly walk—keep it going for a few minutes. Dancing to music will also assist the flow of adrenaline and elevate your heart rate.

These exercises are not mutually exclusive. They blend well and create a more powerful effect when used together. Experiment to see what works best for you.

You are now prepared to start visualizing with chapter 3. Carry the skill of breathwatching with you as you learn to couple it with visualization to achieve what you conceive.

chapter 3

Developing Positive Pictures

One of the more amazing stories to come to us from the POW camps of Vietnam is about a Navy pilot incarcerated for many years. To occupy his time constructively and maintain a form of sanity, he decided to concentrate on learning to play a musical instrument. He had never touched a guitar in his life, and he wasn't about to be presented with one at that time. So he and a buddy drew six lines on a two-inch-wide flat stick (mimicking the neck of a guitar), and presto—a musical instrument that would be the envy of every champion flat-pick guitarist in the world. For the duration of his stay at the "Hanoi Hilton," he compulsively learned to play the guitarlike stick under the tutelage of his cellmate, a professional musician. He would "hear" the sound of certain music and voice it out loud, and his teacher would then show him the appropriate finger position on the neck corresponding to those notes. He memorized the chords and visualized, while in bed, the sequence of actions to produce the desired results. Following years of visualized practice, he was released from prison and returned home as an accomplished guitarist with his sanity intact.

The use of visualization techniques for improved performance is not new, as evidenced by this story. The disciplines of yoga and meditation from ancient India, eastern martial arts, and hypnosis are other examples in which the mind's ability to picture events is an integral aspect of one's physical performance. Where years ago mental training for physical activity was viewed skeptically as hocus-pocus, today visualization and other techniques of training the mind have found their way into all sports arenas, where sophisticated athletes, refusing to leave the outcome of performance to chance, train their minds and bodies for peak performance.

In the world of running, British world-class miler Roger Bannister exemplified the power of visualization as he imagined in his mind the entire race scenario prior to his shattering of the 4-minute barrier. He visualized the process of victory, and refused to accept the images of others and their beliefs about how impossible it would be for a human to run faster than 4 minutes for a mile.

Lee Evans, 1968 Olympic gold medalist in the 400-meter event, also demonstrated the power of mental visualization and the importance of mental training. He mentally prepared each stride of his Olympic performance for two full years before the event took place. He ran one of the most brilliant 400-meter races in Olympic history, clocking 43.86, a world record that stood for 20 years.

National champions Ceci St. Geme (5000 meters) and Regina Jacobs (1500 meters) claim that visualization has helped them realize their full potential. They talk about hearing splits, feeling surges, and sensing other aspects of the race in explicit detail prior to their national championship–winning performances. More recently, Regina has set a new American record for 5000 meters— a new event for her—using visualization and other precepts and tools described throughout this book. What seems to be true across the board is that the athletes who are most successful have constructed the basis for their performances well in advance of the actual moment of competition.

Needless to say, if you fail to train your body, your mind will not perform miracles. Visual training must work in conjunction with top-notch physical training. For example, world-class triathlete Mark Allen, six-time winner of the Hawaiian Ironman events, has always relied on visualization techniques to become mentally strong. With the first race of a particular season one week away, he realized he was not in his best physical shape. Rather than panic, he decided to rely on his mental toughness. Each day leading up to the race, he visualized himself as a strong, powerful athlete, racing like the world's best. When he got to the starting line, he felt terrific. Then the race started and, according to Mark, "Mike Pigg (his closest rival) went out and kicked my butt. So much for visualization." Allen's story points out that if you don't have the strong physical base, no amount of brainpower can create a miracle. Even an athlete as great as Mark Allen cannot rely on his mental training to make up for any lack of physical conditioning.

What Is Visualization?

There is a difference between *visual thinking* and the process of visualization. The former is a random attempt to think about some future event or situation. When left to chance, these thoughts may take the form of negative worry about all of the catastrophic possibilities. Such negative images can create anxiety and fear, wasting your nervous energy, jeopardizing your focus, and thus increasing the probability of undesirable outcomes. Visualiza-

tion, on the other hand, is an active, preplanned attempt to choose appropriate success images while in a deeply relaxed state of mind in order to influence how your body responds to a set of circumstances. It is a learned skill that needs to be practiced regularly in a relaxed state. Running within involves using the process of planned visualization prior to any workout or race; it is an integral facet of the total training program. The mind, therefore, is trained like a muscle. If you wanted to become a strong 10K runner, you wouldn't think of running a workout once a month and expecting results. So, too, if you want a strong mind, you need to work out mentally on a consistent basis.

How Does Visualization Work?

The process of visualization works because it cues the body to synchronize millions of neural and muscular activities in a "dress rehearsal" for upcoming runs or races, much like actors getting ready for a stage production. During this process, you call into play as many of your five senses as possible to help you formulate clear, vivid images. You can *see* yourself perform as well as *feel* the process. *Hearing* the crowd cheer, *smelling* the grass, and *feeling* your foot touch the ground all work. By constant practice of visualization, the pictures developed will be more easily interpreted by the central nervous system as if they were real. The meditative state prior to visualization helps to stop the mind chatter (distractions), clearing the way for you to introduce positive images. Using visualization hand in hand with meditation will help you to focus more sharply on the images being visualized.

Scientists have shown that images have a powerful impact on every cell in our bodies. It is important to understand this phenomenon as a runner. Much of our muscle movement is activated by images; visualization has been shown to create measurable amounts of contraction in those muscles used for specific tasks.

To experience this effect on your muscles, try the following exercise. While lying down, legs uncrossed and out straight, achieve a deep level of relaxation using the breathwatching method described in chapter 2. When totally relaxed, imagine the lower parts of your legs becoming covered with concrete. *See* the concrete being poured; *feel* the coolness and texture. As it dries, notice how it solidifies and encases your legs. Gently try to lift your feet. Don't strain. Notice the heaviness of the concrete and how difficult it is to budge that part of your body. Now reverse the process and imagine the blocks cracking and falling away from your legs. You now have helium balloons tied to your ankles; feel the lightness of your legs as they rise into the air. Notice how your legs move easily in an upward direction.

Aside from its effect on muscles, research is now showing that visualization can actually change blood pressure, heart rate, body temperature, and other functions of the body, processes that ultimately influence your running performance. Visualization is a process that simply quiets and clears the mind of limiting thoughts and stops them from sabotaging your running efforts, so that your body is capable of doing what it has been trained to do. For example, you could be in the best shape of your life, but negative self-talk and images will create anxiety and tension that block your efforts to run according to your capabilities. Positive visualization, however, works to clear the way for you to do all that is needed to be successful. It keeps you on track—focused on running relaxed and controlled—and maximizes your chances of positive results.

Visualization also creates expectations of satisfaction, happiness, and joy, and you respond by choosing the right workout, race strategy, and training program. By rehearsing and focusing with visualization correctly, you not only prepare for your best performance, you also are able to plan for and offset potential speed bumps along the way. For example, visualization can help you to adapt to adverse weather conditions. If the race site typically is windy, you can imagine your body as an aerodynamic wedge that smoothly slips through the wind, unaffected by the force. If the course is particularly hilly, visualize yourself gliding to the top of each hill. Try to anticipate any difficult situation and visually see yourself responding effectively.

Putting Visualization to Use

As we've now discussed the foundations of visualization necessary for optimal running, be prepared for opportunities at the end of each chapter throughout the rest of the book to practice specific visualizations. These visualization exercises reinforce the principles and precepts of becoming the body–mind–spirit runner. By applying this powerful tool as part of your daily running workouts, you will effectively rehearse upcoming competitive events.

You don't have to be an elite runner to benefit from visualization. It works with anyone who commits to the consistency of physical and mental training. Whenever you run, plan to take an extra 10 to 15 minutes prior to your workout or race to find a quiet place, at home or at the race, free of potential interruptions or distractions. Sit or recline in a relaxed position. Close your eyes. Take five deep breaths through your nostrils, hold each breath for approximately five seconds, then slowly release each one. You will, with a little practice, begin to feel very calm. Take about five minutes to get into this relaxed state of mind before visualizing. (It is in this state of mind, remember, that your central nervous system is most receptive to images created in the mind.) Then visualize yourself performing exactly as you would hope.

> In a relaxed state, imagine your legs very relaxed and loose with the tension flowing away. Imagine your body like a fine-tuned machine—upright, smooth, powerful. Click into the start of the workout and see yourself running, light on your feet. Tell yourself, *This is the best I've ever felt . . . wonderful.* Try to imagine various landmarks along the way and see yourself running smoothly and feeling great as you glide up a hill. Tell yourself, *I'm so relaxed and so strong, I could go another few miles.* Notice that the conversation you have with yourself is all positive. As you approach the conclusion of the run, feel yourself finishing strong with energy to spare.

Immediately following this mental training session, open your eyes, stand, and begin to perform according to these images.

Practice visualization daily for a minimum of 10 minutes. Be patient with and persistent in acquiring this skill; it may take a few days to catch on and stay with the visualization without being distracted by other thoughts. Don't get discouraged. In time, you will perfect it and enjoy the benefits.

Many athletes ask, *Isn't it dangerous to get my hopes up by visualizing the positive and risk being disappointed? Maybe I should prepare for the worst and if everything turns out okay, great.* It's true that preparing for negative possibilities will prevent disappointment, but such thinking also contributes to negative outcomes that aren't necessarily inevitable. You can live with disappointment and even learn from it. Why not increase the likelihood of positive results through the use of visualization?

Here are some other interesting exercises we recommend when racing or on leisurely training runs. These mind exercises are enjoyable, and the results are usually immediate. When you become accomplished with them, use those you enjoy most during your next competition or workout.

• In a deeply relaxed state, imagine your next race exactly the way you want to perform. Start with the night before, eating the perfect meal; visualize your body fueling up and sleeping restfully. Feel the excitement of the crowd as you warm up. At the start of the race, begin to run fluidly, smoothly, calmly, and strongly. Imagine feeling this way in the middle of the race and crossing the finish line in good shape. Hear yourself talking to others after the race about how great you felt and how pleased you are with the results.

• While on a run or in a race, let your running partner get in front of you if he seems to have more energy. Imagine a rainbow connecting your heads together, and begin to feel your partner's energy flow through the rainbow into your body.

• As you run into the wind while training or racing, imagine you are shaped like a wedge and cut through the breeze effortlessly.

• Imagine you are a deer, running with grace, style, and strength.

• As you descend off a high hill, look out into the distance and feel like a giant bird, floating to your destination.

• Imagine that your body is a well-greased, highly tuned machine, with all parts moving in synchronicity.

• During a track workout, see yourself floating by the cheering crowds. They all came to see you set a new world record.

Create your own; there are limitless possibilities. Use the same meditation and visualization training skills that you have learned in the preceding pages.

As you embark on this exciting journey of body–mind–spirit fitness, expect to see radical changes as you push the barriers of

what you thought were your limits. You are about to use a greater range of your potential. Actually, each of us possesses greater capability; we just often fail to use it. By visualizing what was previously thought impossible, we make it possible.

Keep in mind that ultimate performances are usually created by your passionate moment-by-moment involvement as you run. You don't dance to get to the other side of the floor; you need not run to get to the end of the workout or race. Enjoy the process and be successful in the moment; true success is measured by the quality of the run, the attention and mindful involvement in each moment. By so doing, you will begin to redefine your running potential and go to new levels of performance—not only in your sport, but in all of life. Remember, in the process of visualization, you are the producer, director, writer, and star of all your imagined scripts. Enjoy the show!

chapter 4

Affirming
Your Greatness

A world-class runner with whom I (Jerry) have worked expressed concern about her ability to make the U.S. Olympic team. The athletes invited to run the qualifying trials comprised the best group of runners ever assembled for that distance. When questioned about her chances, she replied, "I'm not sure that I deserve to be here; there's so much talent in this race that I'm not confident I'll make the team." With a little help, she rephrased her negative monologue to one that would reflect the direction she wished to go. She created new phrases: *I am a member of the women's Olympic team; I deserve to represent my country at the Olympics;* and *I am in position to strike and get what I like.* She recorded these sentences on index cards and carried them with her at all times, reciting each one at least 15 times each day while visualizing them to be true. While marinating her nervous system with these positive statements and directives, her fears subsided and her greatest dream became a reality as she qualified as a member of the U.S. Olympic team. According to ancient Chinese wisdom, the words you choose are the seeds of your future realities. Negative expressions create mental and physical resistance that hinders your efforts; positive words provide the power to transform the quality of your existence and open the floodgates of performance.

On the other hand, negative self-talk can stand in the way of your best performance. Negative putdown messages can disturb your fine-tuned higher cortical brain function that governs your running and mental attitude. Thoughts of self-doubt and decreased self-worth develop into feelings of anxiety and panic as the limbic system arousal colors the thoughts with emotions and feelings.

An athlete participating in the 1988 Seoul Olympics was waiting in the security area preparing to go into the Olympic stadium for her event. Because of the long wait, she started to talk negatively to herself. Due to the relative importance of this competitive event in her career as an elite athlete, she developed a full-blown panic attack. When she finally arrived at the starting line, she was in no condition to perform up to her capability. The negative language had taken its toll.

Physiologically, what took place? This athlete's repeated negative self-talk (from the cortex) is mixed with emotional reactions (from the limbic system's hypothalamus and thalamus). These powerful emotions can stimulate images that reinforce the process until it snowballs out of control. The pressure to perform well and the possibility that she would not, set off a hysterical reaction. This shows up as the classic fight-or-flight reaction, which the limbic system controls. Rational thought from the higher cortex is essentially ignored by the more primitive limbic system, which takes charge and controls your behavior.

The Power of Affirmations

It is crucial to remember that we are incapable of thinking poorly while performing our best. The brain (and the limbic system) must ensure the survival of the species. Imagine a zebra or gazelle running away from a lion or cheetah and suddenly thinking, *I'm not fast enough to escape; I'd better just stop running now.* In nature, all prey run their best to avoid their predators. Now picture the lion or cheetah running along and suddenly thinking, *I'm no good, I can't fight this zebra. I'll just give up now.* It is obvious that the drive to fight or flee must be powerful, decisive, and accurate; there is no room for ambiguity.

Humans, however, are capable of creating ambiguity by letting negative images seep in. This creates confusion between the mind and body, resulting in a less than desirable response and performance. Affirmations, on the other hand, are direct attempts to change patterns of negativity that continue to repeat themselves like a broken record.

As we define it, *affirm* means *to make firm* by using conscious, preplanned, and positive words and expressions that help to keep you on track. Without them, the possibility of desirable outcomes diminishes. Unlike visualizations, which control what you "see," affirmations control what you say and think. They are words that give you permission to open up to your greatness and abilities within your sport, the way it was meant to be. To notice the power of words, recite out loud the following two scenarios as if they were true.

> *I am an over-the-hill, out-of-shape, worthless runner who doesn't deserve to be here in this race with all these athletes.*

*I am a strong, vibrant, talented, physically fit runner
who deserves the opportunity to realize my greatness as
an athlete.*

You can't help but feel excited, hopeful, motivated, courageous,
and confident when uttering the latter words of strength. These
feelings generated by the positive affirmations will enable you to
relax, free of anxiety and tension, thus clearing the path for
optimal performance.

Now try the following experiment to experience the difference
in performance as a result of negative and positive self-talk. Run
a mile on the track to warm up. Stretch your body. Now run 4 ×
400 meters, accelerating on the straightaways (100 meters each)
while jogging the turns. Time how long it takes to run each
straightaway, and alternate positive and negative self-talk for each
straightaway. For example, on the first 100 sprint, say over and
over, *I'm fast, smooth, and strong.* On the very next one, repeat a
phrase such as *I'm a slow, lazy slug.* Notice the difference in how
you feel and how fast you run.

Try the following test with a friend: hold your arm out straight
while a friend tries to push it down. Resist the pressure as you say
out loud, *I love running hills,* over and over. Now change the
phrase to *I hate hills,* and have your friend push again. Compare
the strength you experience. Notice how much stronger you are,
and how much better your performance is, when you vocalize *I
love*—a positive thought pattern. How many of us, consciously or
not, have a love–hate relationship with various aspects of training
and racing? You love the outcome of working out, but hate the
process. If you say you hate running hills, you'll create more
tension and anxiety, making it more difficult to get to the top.
Better to say *I love running up hills; they get me into better shape
on my way to becoming a better competitor.* In this way, you begin
to see their advantage, and you will experience rising up the hill
rather than forcing your way there.

This exercise was tested at Penn State University with head
track coach Harry Groves and his cross-country team. In the midst
of their season, they were looking for ways to exhibit their
presence and exert their power over an All-American archrival in
a regional meet. The mighty Nittany Lions were talented and
strong, yet were overly concerned about the difficult hills that
awaited them on that Saturday morning. They talked about loving

the hills as partners for gaining an advantage. *We love hills* became their affirmation. At mile 4 in the contest, it was anyone's race— until the words *We love hills, we love hills* were echoed by Coach Groves standing at the foot of the most gruesome hill. In a split-second, upon hearing these words, the Nittany Lions roared past all their competitors, running away with a sweet victory.

Before we go any further, we can hear some of you raising an objection. Some of you find it difficult to affirm something that may not be true in the moment. You feel deceitful affirming, *I am a strong, fast runner,* when it may not be so today. However, saying these words will keep your feet pointed in the right direction and keep you motivated to do all that's required to reach this goal. Even if you fall short, you will still be farther along the path than you would be if you hadn't affirmed your direction in this way. We shouldn't be afraid to open up to the vast possibilities of life and enjoy the process. Remember that affirmations are simply *self-direction*, not *self-deception*.

What Makes a Good Affirmation?

There are some important steps that you must take to form workable, powerful affirmations for positive self-talk. Use these guidelines:

- Keep the phrase short, concise, specific, and simple.
- Keep it positive; affirm what you want, not what you don't want.
- Use present tenses. Frame your statements as if the future were now. Rather than say *I will finish in the top 10,* say *I finish in the top 10.* Act as if it were true, and it will keep you on track.
- Be consistent. Recite affirmations aloud each day for a few minutes instead of once a week for an hour. Do this as part of your 10- to 15-minute meditation and visualization sessions, and "see" what the words say.
- Use rhythm. A cadence or rhyme will help you to remember the affirmations more easily. For example: *I'm in position to strike and get what I like.*

Once you know the rules, you are then ready to apply them to constructing your personal affirmations. We suggest that you start by developing two lists—one with five running goals, and one with five negative statements that you typically recite in relation to your performance.

First, take each goal and change it into a positive statement of direction. For example, your short-term goal is to overcome your fear of hills. Affirm: *I love hills . . . they are my friends.* It may even help to think of reasons why you should love hills—for example, running hills is a positive event because it significantly improves conditioning as an athlete. By thinking in this way, you have a distinct mental advantage over opponents who continue to hate them.

Now take a few of your negative self-talk statements and turn them around. *I never improve* becomes *Better and better every day in every way.* Change *I can't surge* to *I continue to improve my ability to surge.*

In running—as in all sporting activities—affirmations are quite useful in turning fear into confidence, improving your concentration, reducing self-criticism, sharpening your biomechanical skills, helping you cope with fatigue, and focusing on any other performance tasks that may need attention. Simply follow the rules and tailor the phrase to your particular needs.

Putting Affirmations to Use

We suggest that you write each individual affirmation on a three-by-five-inch index card; carry them around in a pack to read when you have time, and place them strategically in areas that you frequently visit during the day: the bathroom mirror, the refrigerator door, the dashboard of your car, or next to the telephone. Recite the phrases out loud to yourself whenever you notice them. Incorporate them with your daily visualization sessions as another component of your 10- to 15-minute mental training program. After you recite each one, close your eyes and picture what the words are saying. For example, if your affirmations are *I run with ease like a tireless deer* or *I am a strong, aggressive competitor who is capable of great things,* see yourself being this way in a race; feel what it would be like to win a race in your category or just run well.

Here are some other affirmations that may resonate with you. Use these and create more of your own. Each of the following chapters will present you with specific sample affirmations that will help you solidify the principles that will help you to become a body–mind–spirit dancing runner.

> *Lean and trim, I run to win.*
>
> *Calm and confident, I run well.*
>
> *Good competitors are gifts, enabling me to run my best.*
>
> *I may or may not win, but I run like a well-trained athlete.*
>
> *Health is me; I'm injury free.*
>
> *Fatigue is the necessary step in exploring my full potential.*
>
> *When I relax my jaw, I achieve so much more.*
>
> *All things come to those who wait . . . I persist each day in every way.*

I gain without strain.

I look for ways to bring more pleasure to my run.

Running is my guide to a healthier, happier life.

I give myself permission to rest when it's best.

   Let affirmations be the vehicle that carries you away from false self-messages and into closer range with your true potential—who you really are, and what is possible given your true self. Affirmations are the language of possibility and change; their purpose is to remove the static, limiting impressions of the mind and to create a more unlimited, expansive sense of what can be. Affirmations are geared toward the awakening of each of us to our potentialities rather than the limitations of life.

   Remember, within the rose at all times is its full potential. It is constantly in the process of change and growth as it comes into its own. When we give it water, sun, and nourishment, it blossoms fully. Like this flower, you are a natural unfolding athlete. Nurture yourself with encouragement and positive affirmations (avoiding the messages that kill your spirit). You have all that you need within you now to become all that you can be. Simply notice it, and affirm it to be so.

   Now that you have finished part I, you have set the foundation of the body–mind–spirit runner with the mental skills of relaxation, visualization, and affirmation. Practice them consistently and diligently each day that you work out physically. When you do, you will immediately notice your relationship with running changing and growing in a dynamic way. The remaining chapters will give you ample opportunity to apply your newly acquired skills. Have fun on the journey into the mind as you become the runner you deserve to be.

II

Restructuring Attitudes for True Success

For many athletes, the sport of distance running has been characterized by certain competitive attitudes: Run hard, run to win, run to own your opponent. Billy Mills, in the movie *Running Brave*, slows at the finish well ahead of his nearest competitor. His coach screams, "Take him for everything," intimating that the victory is not enough; he must crush his opponent. Although winning is important, there is so much more.

In part II, we examine traditional approaches to competition, as we did in chapter 1 with motivation and goals, and offer alternative attitudes, mind-sets that help you to focus energy away from the products, results, and outcomes toward the process—your moment-to-moment involvement each step of the way. By so doing, you have the opportunity to transcend the ordinary and sense an inner freedom that will propel you to greater heights, extraordinary experiences in every aspect of running performance.

Running offers so much more than an outcome. Runners know this, and are beginning to search for ways to restructure their attitudes. The shifts in consciousness presented in part II will help you to see running as a way to face external challenges as well as accept the challenges within, where the opponent is yourself on your inward-bound journey toward ultimate running.

In chapter 5, you will learn about inner virtues such as self-knowledge, modesty, simplicity, centeredness, and persistence that will help you rise to new levels of performance as you decrease the pressure, tension, and anxiety that accompany most competition situations. In chapter 6, you will begin to embrace risks as you stare the fear of failure in the face, poised to learn from all setbacks and forge ahead as a more accomplished athlete. Notice in chapter 7 that your opponent is actually a gift, a partner on the path to excellence. Finally, in chapter 8, you deserve to learn the most powerful paradox in athletics: let go of the need to win and be victorious. Winning and victory are often felt but not seen. Learn how to redefine victory, and you will experience winning every time you race.

chapter 5

Exhibiting the Warrior Within

Following his stunning victory at the New York City Marathon, Kenyan runner Douglas Wakiihuri talked about how he floated effortlessly over the course with dominating ease. With Zen simplicity he spoke of the marathon as sacred ground, ripe with the fruit of life's truths. When sports journalists asked him about the traditional concerns runners usually have about mileage, fitness level, racing strategy, and diet, he quickly pointed out how such a journey deserves better; there's so much more that this race offers each of us, particularly the chance to confront fear, fatigue, failure, patience, perseverance, courage, confidence, ego, self-doubt, and a host of other concerns within each of us. Douglas was exhibiting his deeper essence as a warrior runner by bringing our attention to a new level of awareness beyond running itself to a place where our external successes and accomplishments in sport are the mere reflections of those victories within.

The way of the warrior runner is no different than the Japanese Samurai or Native American Vision Quest. Such warriors were individualistic, courageous, focused, visionary, modest, passionate, and they competed for a higher good beyond their own self-interest in order to rise to new levels of achievement and extraordinary performance. They were athletes of indomitable spirit and iron will, who knew that all was possible by believing in themselves. These warriors were specialists in defeating an opponent when the true battle had little to do with external events and much to do with the battles within. They were fierce competitors who waged war against their inner fears, and the rewards for victory were deeply personal.

So it is for all of us who run with the warrior spirit; we discover verities about life and ourselves that we never knew existed. Like the ancient warrior, you learn from your workouts and races all you need to know in order to reach your full potential as an athlete, and beyond for the bigger race of life.

Runners who possess this warrior attitude demonstrate very distinct characteristics. The warrior runner . . .

- has courage to risk failure, learn from setbacks, and forge ahead;
- possesses a multidimensional approach to competition;
- focuses on the process as opposed to the outcome (product);
- uses a race to gain greater self-realization;

- knows her weaknesses and trains to strengthen them;
- sees competitors as partners who facilitate improvement;
- understands that racing is a roller coaster and learns patience to ride the ups and downs; and
- enjoys running for the pleasure it gives.

An athlete who repeatedly demonstrated this new warrior attitude was professional triathlete Mark Allen, legendary Ironman champion. In what was his final race before retirement, the "King of Kona" found himself trailing the leader by an almost insurmountable 13 minutes going into the marathon. Yet he never gave up; his challenge was totally within. In what many consider to be the greatest comeback performance in racing history, Allen—nicknamed "The Grip" because his opponents said that when he is chasing them down, they feel his presence gripping them—passed Tom Hellriegel during the marathon with 3 miles left. This earned Allen his sixth Ironman win.

According to Allen, every race is a teacher, showing you how to win in many different ways. There were many opportunities for Mark to learn how to win prior to his six victories. In 1982 he did not finish. In 1983 he finished third. In 1984 he had a 12-minute lead starting the run, yet blew up and faded to fifth. In 1986 and 1987, he pushed hard, yet finished second both times. In 1989, he returned and raced head to head with Dave Scott for 140 miles, and then, surging over the last 1.5 miles, he broke Scott for his first victory. Allen claims that "The race is so real, it's just you against yourself . . . a very pure experience, very enriching." This is the attitude of the warrior runner.

To become a warrior runner, begin to challenge your opponent with magical weapons—inner virtues that help you to fight less to win than to demonstrate your composure under the pressure of combat; where you choreograph a harmonious dance between your self, the terrain, and the competition to create more fun and enhance your performance with each run. Develop and nurture the following ways of the warrior.

Self-Knowledge

This is the most powerful weapon of the warrior runner. Knowing the terrain and your competitors is necessary, but this knowledge must be accompanied by self-knowledge—an accurate appraisal of your physical, mental, and emotional fitness. The warrior runner has the courage to take an accurate inventory of the struggles, blockages, obstacles, and fears, and to determine where the most work is needed in order to improve.

Also, knowing one's true self is a hedge against selling out. As a warrior, you don't want to give your competitors permission to make you feel inferior. Refuse to compromise your talents, toughness, strengths, and courage; run with integrity. Show up to demonstrate what you do have as an athlete, and feel proud of that. Trust the power within and use it; when you don't, that's when fear sets in. Do not compromise your integrity; remember that you are good enough, and you deserve to be the best you can be. Regardless of any other competitor, you have value, something to contribute. Begin to display all of your attributes as an athlete. All else is irrelevant.

Steadiness

It is crucial for the warrior to be steady and free of emotional upheaval while running. To do this, settle and calm the mind through daily meditation, visualization, and affirmations. To help in this regard, enter your relaxed state with breathwatching skills. While relaxed, try to visualize your performance as you would like it to be—perfect. Open your eyes and carry this state of body and mind into your activity. Notice how composed and focused you are, able to run your very best. Steady, even pacing over the entire distance is the key to top performances. For races longer than 10 minutes, the final 2 minutes can be a final kick. Races shorter than 10 minutes may also include a kick; however, in the most effective races, the duration of the kick is usually 30 seconds or less. If you are kicking before this time, then you may need to reevaluate your pacing during the race; it may be time to quicken your overall race pace a notch.

No matter what the distance, though, completing the first half of the race in 50 to 52 percent of your overall predicted finish and the second half in 48 to 50 percent of your expected finish will most likely give you your best results timewise.

Modesty

When you compete as a runner, there is always a danger of becoming too self-involved, smitten with your prowess or level of fitness. The opportunities to display your wares, make claims, and boast are readily available. However, the code of the warrior states that the more you try to look good in the eyes of others, the farther you separate yourself from your integrity. Too much egocentric behavior ultimately creates battles within, leading to diminished confidence and much self-doubt.

When you begin to experience self-absorption, switch back to a more modest place. Remind yourself that humility and an attitude of unassuming modesty bring greater success and less embarrassment over time, particularly when you fall short of your impossible-to-live-up-to predictions. Notice how running can humble you when you least expect it. Knowing this should help you not get too carried away with your prowess. This is not to say that you cannot be proud of your achievement; be a hero on the podium and cherish the moment of victory. Celebrate your efforts while recognizing that bragging and self-illumination are the patterns of insecure athletes who need to promote themselves, yet find it difficult to live up to this inflated image. For most of us, keeping our egos in check is a battle worth fighting—and winning.

To have honor and glory, be humble and give recognition to the greatness of those around you. Because of them, you are given the opportunity to be your best. Others will be more inclined to recognize your greatness in a sincere fashion when you model the way. Greatness for all of us is a give-and-take proposition. Focusing solely on your own accomplishments is a surefire way to alienate others.

Simplicity

The warrior seeks inner victory through simplicity. According to the warrior, *less is more*. Over the years, we have noticed how complex the sport of distance running has become, as if more is better. Most of us tend to be overly concerned about having the right stuff—watches, shoes, heart monitor, clothing—and lose touch with the beauty and essence of simply running. *Runner's World* editor and author Joe Henderson once said, "Don't let the planning and analyzing interfere with the doing and enjoying." He is so right.

Years ago, American distance star Mark Nenow set a national record in the 10,000-meter run and attributed his victory to the precepts of simplicity. In an age of high-tech and sophisticated physiological feedback equipment, Mark embraced a less complicated way, virtually avoiding scientific training programs. He ran while "listening" to the natural messages of his body.

And who can forget the image of world-class marathoner Bill Rodgers as he crossed the finish line in his first-ever Boston victory? His simple, plain white T-shirt with the initials of his track club printed on the front with a marker didn't blemish his success as he set a course record in the process.

Another famous marathoner, Ethiopian Abebe Bikila, won an Olympic gold medal in the marathon and other victories running barefoot. Fancy clothing and digitally timed runner's watches were not part of his world. He simply ran.

What the warrior teaches is that the greatest happiness and the most extraordinary performances in life come during times of pure simplicity. Avoid complexity and the anxiety and pressure that can accompany it.

Centeredness

When attacked by hostile weather patterns, a deep-rooted tree withstands them, remaining unmoved by the harsh force. So it is with the warrior runner, who remains centered, steady, and unmoved like a tree when confronted by harsh external forces such as failure, mistakes, and setbacks. The warrior refuses to measure his self-worth as a runner by results or outcomes. The centered champion sees all aspects of racing as a process of learning from mistakes, correcting them, and emerging as a more refined runner. The best athletes in the world have missed the winner's circle numerous times before reaching champion status. They have a high tolerance for setbacks, and this keeps them centered on the path to personal excellence. Think about this: everything you've learned about running has been a long road of trial and error.

When you accept mistakes and loss as part of the experience, you are freer to extend yourself, to keep trying, and to take the necessary calculated risks to become great. Down days are opportunities for improvement. Accepting this will help you to relax and stay centered, the keys to running success. The code of the warrior states that when we "lose" or don't meet our goals on the first try, we still profit from this experience. We always strive to win; yet if we fall short, we accept it as part of the risk in trying.

Persistence

The warrior runner knows that deliberate, slow cultivation is the path to success and good fortune. Realizing your goals and attaining success are the by-products of persistence and perspiration. Talent accounts for a mere 5 percent of most achievements. Those runners who appear to have much talent were once struggling beginners. It was persistence and hard work that led them to achievement and excellence.

There is an expression among cyclists: *All is possible—you just need time in the saddle.* Becoming proficient as a runner requires years of training, hours of riding, and persistence through setbacks. It usually takes about 5 years of consistent training before you come into your own as a runner. However, know that you continue to improve for at least 10 years from the moment you initiate a running program, no matter how old you are when you begin. Naturally, this assumes that you are committed to a seasonally and yearly progressive training program. Every dog has his day; you just need to keep at it. The problem with many good athletes is that they are willing to give up just as the palm trees of the oasis begin to appear on the horizon. Giving up is not part of the warrior's lexicon; persistence and consistency in training are.

Integrity

Here is the cornerstone that the warrior runner uses to maintain inner success. Integrity is the constant and consistent refusal to compromise your talents, abilities, and sense of self.

So many runners compromise their integrity by turning away from their true selves and giving up because of intimidation and fear. In so doing, they give other competitors permission to make them feel inferior, undeserving, or less than they are. Warriors resist this.

At a national championship race, I (Jerry) was in command, leading a pack of athletes whom I had not been expected to beat. As I ran the race of my life, thoughts of doom entered my mind.

Maybe they know something that I don't, I thought. *Am I crazy out here alone? Why don't they lead? They're better runners.* Finally, I caught my negativity and told myself, *I'm great, too. That's why I was invited to run. I deserve to win.* I held on to my integrity and outkicked all but one for a stellar second-place finish in this event.

Follow this example, and feel your power as a runner. Know that you are a winner when you exhibit your integrity as a warrior, even if the results don't show it. Whether you're the favorite or the underdog, ahead or behind, you can stay in touch with your integrity by focusing not on the outcome, but on your willingness to exhibit your level of fitness.

When confronted by fear of an opponent or the possibility of failure, do not compromise what you possess as a runner. Deal with the situation by exhibiting the ability you do have rather than fighting the force head-on. Simply do what you can do. Show yourself and others your greatness, even if you are less powerful than your opponent. Remember that *you* are good enough. You deserve the best, so act as if this were true. Regardless of anyone else's position, you have value, something to demonstrate, something to teach. You deserve the opportunity to display your level of fitness when it is time.

As you can see, the code of the warrior runner is based on the attainment of inner success. You, too, can be a warrior if you focus on what these virtues mean to you and exhibit your own level of greatness. As a warrior runner, you must possess your own sense of what achievement is for you; setting your own goals that matter to you is crucial. The warrior knows that once inner success is achieved, there is less need for external victory; and with less need for external victory, there is less tension, anxiety, and pressure to win. And, with less anxiety and tension, it is easier for the relaxed warrior to achieve external victory, the by-product of the successful inner journey. Let external victory be the mere reflection of the triumph within.

When you begin to adopt these virtues of the warrior, you will notice an overall decrease in the pressure, tension, and anxiety that accompany all competitive situations. Such changes will have a positive effect on your performance and provide a deeper appreciation of your sport. As a warrior runner, show up at the races knowing that your training is as complete as it can be for now. Simply perform like the well-trained runner you are. Don't obsess about outcomes or results; set your body free to do what it does best, what you have trained it to do. Free of judgment or criticism, let the mind dance with what the body already knows how to do from all the miles of running. Enjoy the dance, the flow, the process. Feel the passion you have for this graceful sport. Refuse to focus on anything but the joy and the fun of a well-executed plan.

Visualization

Become totally relaxed, using the breathwatching technique described in chapter 2. Close your eyes and visualize the following.

Feel yourself running a race.

Notice all of the spectators and competitors.

Feel yourself as you focus on the flow of the run.

Sense your confidence building as the miles go by.

Experience the end as you run according to race plans.

Visualize the finish and feel the exhilaration from performing so well.

Affirmations

Use these in conjunction with visualization, and create your own in the blanks.

I am a courageous, passionate, fearless warrior runner.

My success as a warrior runner is the reflection of my victories within.

I simply perform like the well-trained runner I am.

_____

_____

_____

chapter 6

Becoming Courageous on the Run

So many of us have grown up in a world where winning isn't everything—it's the only thing. In Atlanta during the 1996 Olympics, billboard ads promoted the idea that *You don't win the silver; you lose the gold.* No wonder we have such obsessive fears over the possibility of failing. And as long as we nurture this fear, it affects our performances as a self-fulfilling prophecy: the very thing we fear—failure—comes to fruition. The fear itself is directly responsible for the multitude of deleterious physiological responses that the body generates to protect itself from the fright, yet this fear hinders the body's ability to fluently perform. When afraid, you become tense, tight, less fluid, and incapable of making good decisions. Vasoconstriction (closing of the arterial pathways) limits the flow of blood to the brain, which impedes your ability to think clearly. As a result, you lose your focus and make tactical errors while performing.

To help yourself overcome this limiting fear, consider shifting your attitude to become a bold, audacious athlete courageous enough to stare the fear of failure in the face, regardless of how insecure that may feel. Traditional attitudes toward failure often prevent us from going for it to become our best, thus depriving us of the opportunity to discover the limitless boundaries of our potential. Rather than bypass the chance for success by avoiding potential failure situations, see your most important successes in life as the result of learning from your biggest failures, making the corrections, and forging ahead.

Chinese wisdom reminds us that we lose, and in learning from this come out ahead. Failure is a necessary step toward ultimately reaching such success. As we define it, true failure is the unwillingness to take the risks to grow and become a better runner. By adopting this shift in consciousness, we can become courageous runners and open up to so much more. By giving ourselves permission to fail, we can discover our greatness. In the extrinsic success-oriented world of running, loss, failure, mistakes, errors, and setbacks initially seem to be abominations to be avoided at all costs. However, once we realize that avoidance of such outcomes is impossible and that they in fact contribute to our ultimate successes, we can relax and accept what's natural. If you're honest with yourself, you know that it's futile to avoid failure, because it's inevitable. The more you race, the more you realize that you can influence the outcome but you can't control it.

When consulting with some of this nation's best runners, we notice they share many common traits, one of which is the courage to learn from setbacks. They accept and tolerate failure as a necessary ingredient in the performance pie, the price paid for taking the risks to improve. A full, enjoyable, exciting life as a runner, one in which you push the limits of your personal and physical potential, will always include thousands of risks and failures. Great runners fear failure just like everyone else, but they go ahead anyway because they have the courage to follow their hearts and do what they instinctively know is right. In fact, the word courage is taken from the French word *coeur*, meaning *heart*.

Perhaps you've heard the axiom *The arrow that hits the bull's-eye is the result of a hundred misses.* Similarly, you perfect your running through adversity and failure. Three-time Olympic gold medalist Jackie Joyner-Kersee has held 19 world records in various track-and-field events. She was not always a winner, and claims that losing a race and understanding why allowed her to become the champion she is. In a sense, her tolerance for failure allowed it to become her friend, her teacher, and her guru. In this way, the fear vanishes and performance is enhanced.

As competitive runners, we often experience setbacks while running important races. Each experience we have yields us a treasure of knowledge, if we choose to see and accept it that way. The lesson here is to redirect failure and setback so that they work for you, not against you.

Going to Running School

If you needed to grasp the art of archery to hunt for food in order to live, you would do so—step by step, learning by trial and error. If you made a mistake in the process of learning, you'd seek advice to remedy the situation and have the courage to try again until you became proficient—no blame, no embarrassment, no failure. So why not view your running similarly? A race is like going to running school. It's an opportunity to add new dimensions to your race strategies and tactics for better performance. Dwelling on the outcome interferes with your collection of valuable experimental data that could contribute to better performance in the future.

The Chinese character for our word *crisis* has two distinct meanings. On the one hand it indicates *danger*; it also means *opportunity.* In every race crisis situation, there is an opportunity to improve if you look past the ephemeral, and often meaningless, outcome. Put aside your disappointing results—you can't produce a personal record in every race. Instead of the quantitative results, look at how you ran the race. Perhaps it was a fantastic success with respect to even pacing; maybe you were tactically sharp. These are no small achievements. If a mistake was made by going out too slowly, how does that change future performance strategy? Ask yourself the question, *What might I have done differently to run more effectively?* In a relaxed state, visualize the race and rerun it with your newly learned information. Remember to learn from the negative and then throw it away and introduce the positive. Hold on to all that worked well.

It might be helpful to record in your logbook those things that you have learned and what changes you plan to make in the future to improve your training and racing. This will reinforce the lessons you have learned and teach you to turn those negative experiences into positive learning opportunities. For example, you may write next to the quantitative information about a race: *At mile 23 of the marathon, my body seemed heavy and extremely tired. I didn't think I could finish. Mentally, I relaxed by taking a few deep breaths, and told myself to run just for 100 meters. When I did, I realized at that moment that I could do this to the finish— and I did. I learned that sometimes effort is mind over matter.* Such an entry could be the basis of future successes. Other entries could comment on how the physical coincided with your prerace visualization; how you were able to cope with failure during a race; how you feel about yourself after a certain workout; or how your performance mirrored your affirmations.

Becoming Courageous

To help yourself become more courageous, begin to see the opportunity in every crisis. When you have a major failure, go through the following six steps to help you regain your perspective and to learn from the setback:

1. Record the objective facts about the situation; for example, *I dropped out two miles from the finish.*

2. Record your subjective judgment about this experience; for example, *I'm a terrible runner, a loser. I don't deserve to be here.*

3. Record your feeling with response to this subjective judgment; for example, *I'm devastated, depressed, and upset.*

4. Record the objective data that supports the judgment in step 2. There is probably no conclusive physical data to verify your comments.

5. Record what you've learned from the setback; for example, *I need to focus on hill repeats in my training and pace myself better at the start.*

6. Record how you feel based on step 5. For example: *I'm still disappointed, but I'll be okay. I'm a better runner because of it and I look forward to my next race.*

In addition to this strategy, use the following attitudinal shifts to help you become more courageous and see failure and setback as necessary, positive, inevitable processes on your path to becoming your best as a runner.

• To set the stage for success and minimize the occurrence of failure, establish realistic but challenging short-term goals. Because you are likely to achieve these goals frequently, you will build in the psychological message that you are a winner and you can accomplish your goals. This will ignite courage, confidence, motivation, and commitment for future directions.

• Remember that failure is part of the process of successful running. Performance is a roller coaster; to think otherwise is irrational and will cause you much stress and discouragement. Lighten up on yourself. Ups and downs can be expected. The performance of most serious runners fluctuates by the week. You win some, you lose some; some days you're hot, some days you're not. Don't fight with yourself when failure, the teacher, pays an unexpected visit. Open up to learning from it.

• Mastery in running is the result of consistent physical and mental training. The effects are cumulative. Give yourself the time, however long, to come into your own. Patience, persistence, and perseverance are the three virtues of extraordinary performance. Remember that, for most of us, it takes years to come into our own. Overnight development is quite rare. Most have paid their dues waiting for the time when it all comes together.

• Failure is not devastating, but it is disappointing. When you look back on outward success or failures in competitive situations, you'll notice that they're rarely indicative of absolute truth: you are never as great as your best victory or as bad as your worst defeat. Realistically, neither are accurate indicators of your full potential. Refuse to give too much credence to your ephemeral results.

• In aikido, the fighter blends with the direction of an opposing force, moves with it, and uses it to her advantage. Try this approach with failure: see it as an opposing force; accept it and blend with it, using its lessons to your advantage. By so doing, the power of the opposing force (failure) ceases to exist. You redirect the force and forge ahead.

- You must be willing to lose before you can win. You never want to look back with regret over your competitive days and wish you had taken the risk to go all-out and find how good you really were. If you just do, you'll continue to improve.

Strengthening Through Taking Risks

Running marathons always presented me (Jerry) with plenty of opportunities to test my courage. When I was running with the lead pack at mile 10 in the Summit Marathon in California, I decided to put it on the line and surge into the front. This move was risky, because a surge so early in a 26.2-mile event could cause muscle cramping, oxygen debt, rapid burning of glycogen fuel, and a host of other potential physiological problems. Yet by doing it, I psychologically demoralized my competitors, established myself as a frontrunner, and eventually won the race. Moreover, taking this tactical risk helped me in every subsequent race by strengthening my competitive courage as well as improving my performance.

Taking risks makes you inwardly strong, instilling in you a profound awareness, adding new meaning and richness to your running and racing; taking risks usually leads to breakthroughs in your running. When most runners are asked how they improve, they say it's their willingness to go out on a limb with the courage to take risks and learn from the outcome, whether favorable or not.

But what kind of risks are we talking about? There are as many types of risks as there are runners. For some, cutting back on professional work to train more diligently is a big risk, yet necessary if you're going to become a serious contender on the race circuit. Taking tactical chances during a race—such as going out hard from the start or surging at a certain point—are risks that can affect you both physically and emotionally. You may go into oxygen debt when you surge up that hill, and you may look foolish in front of your peers if you "fail." Then there's the risk that all of us face in our lives, the subtle risk of never taking steps to improve and never answering the question, *What if I had competed on the edge?* Risking regret for the rest of your life is the worst risk of all.

To help yourself create the courage to take risks, follow these five steps in order.

1. Ask yourself: *Will taking this risk possibly improve my running performance?* If yes, go to step 2. If the answer is no and it won't help your running performance, there's probably no point in taking the risk.

2. What is your worst-case scenario for taking the risk? If you can accept this outcome, go for it. If not, put the risk on hold; stay within your comfort zone and wait until your skills or confidence improve. It is vital that you learn what's important and what's not.

3. If you decide to take the risk, be sure to plan a detailed program, obtaining information and instruction that will facilitate your performance. Remember that if you fail to plan, you plan to fail.

4. After the risk is taken, regardless of the outcome, be sure to congratulate yourself for having the courage to have taken the risk. Know that in time, taking repeated risks will ultimately lead to success, and that without risking you will not succeed.

5. The final step is to study the outcome of the risk. What did you learn? How will this help you? Was it all that difficult in retrospect? Based on this, what risks do you have planned for the future? Risks raise many questions; that's why this running journey is a quest. The answers provide the path that you'll choose along the way.

Working with professional and elite athletes in many sports has taught us that taking a risk usually pays off—if not the first time it is taken, then in subsequent times or in what is learned from taking the risk. Using the above steps, a mountain biker decided to take a risk in a race to bolster her confidence during a discouraging season. Prior to the race, she visualized the plan and imagined herself successfully completing the move, clearing a challenging jump. During the event, she executed the move precisely as planned and took the lead for good, renewing her confidence for the rest of the season. In fact, to her it made the whole season a success.

Physiologically, we remind you to be vigilant with respect to your fluid levels, carbohydrate status (utilization and storage), fatigue factor, and other data that are essential to your decisions to take risks. You want to be sensible and not risk injury and burnout; too much, too soon, too hard is an invitation to disaster.

Keeping Perspective

Keep perspective whenever you face any kind of setback. You are probably in excellent shape compared to the overall population. You've realized tremendous physiological benefits from your running, and your becoming tense over a poor performance negates much of what you have gained. You've come a long way. Not only are a few failures and setbacks inaccurate indications of your abilities and potential, they very well may be the key to your greatest breakthroughs and successes. Put it on the line, be courageous, take the risk to fail, and experience success. Avoiding such a risk may seem emotionally safe at first, but in the long run it will be there to haunt you. Today's failure won't matter in 10 years, but failing to go for it might.

Remember that what's lost by not trying and what's lost by not succeeding are two very different things. In the latter case, you can learn from the setback, and eventually you will get closer to your goal. If you do suffer a setback, use a clear head to go beyond it and to see failure as the cost of being vibrantly alive. See it as a gift to help you become a great runner. As you may know, there are many boats in the water, yet only the courageous go out to sea. You cannot discover new horizons unless you are courageous enough to leave the harbor.

Visualization

Using the skill of breathwatching, become totally relaxed. Then, close your eyes and visualize the following.

Imagine a race or run where you would like to try something new. Perhaps you will go out quickly or slowly this time; surge at a certain point; run even splits; or stay with the lead pack.

Feel your nervousness and anxiety, feelings associated with the risk.

Sense the feeling of relaxation coming over you as you decide the risk is worth taking based on the five steps for courage to risk.

Imagine the scenario as it unfolds exactly as planned.

Feel excited as you complete the run with success, according to your prerace objectives.

Feel the deep satisfaction from having courage to take the risk.

Affirmations

Use these while visualizing; create your own in the blanks and recite them often.

Failures are lessons, helping me to constantly improve.

Risks are a natural way to stay alive with running.

The runners I most admire take the risks that the sport requires.

Temporary loss equals long-term gain.

Setbacks lead to inner strength. I'm a better, more courageous runner as a result.

_____

_____

chapter 7

Competing Is a Partnership

The attitude is pervasive at all levels of performance in today's competitive world. You are expected to compete with the killer instinct; you must be willing to crush your opponent. To compete means to be angry enough at the opposition that you sacrifice nothing in bringing about his demise. Your opponent is the enemy, and the goal is to annihilate him through fierce psychological tactics. Although this approach seems to motivate some, it is actually physiologically counterproductive. Whenever we're about to do harm to others intentionally, our bodies experience an excess of tension and stress that interferes with the fluidity of the muscles, stride, and overall efficiency of performance. Intense feelings of anger, hostility, or rage release high levels of stress hormones from the brain and adrenal glands. These stress hormones elevate your heart rate and energy utilization during exercise, and, in turn, make your effort seem harder. These intense feelings of overpowering others take away from your ability to concentrate; they dilute your energy and ultimately lead to suboptimal performance.

Focusing on diminishing others to appear greater than you are is a waste of time and energy. We know that some athletes use anger to motivate themselves, insisting that they perform better because of it. Of course, they'll never know whether they could improve upon their good performances unless they are willing to see things differently. Physiologically, we know the deleterious effects of anger on the body's ability to perform optimally.

Seek Together

Interestingly enough, when you trace the derivation of the verb *to compete,* you discover that it comes from the Latin word *competere,* which means *to seek together.* We have lost the true meaning of the word. You may remember the story about Jesse Owens, world-record holder in the long jump, who during the 1936 Olympics was on the verge of elimination after fouling on his first two attempts. Listening to a timely suggestion from his closest competitor, Owens made the necessary technical adjustment in his approach stride, which enabled him to win the gold medal in the process. Because Owens remained in the competition, his opponent

went on to jump his best ever; overjoyed at that, he walked out of the stadium with Owens, arm in arm. By competing with one another, we help one another seek together to do our individual best, to push us to greater heights than we might be able to achieve on our own.

I (Jerry) can remember competing in a national 15K cross-country championship race in Houston, Texas. Many of the runners were talking about the ways they could defeat their closest rivals. They alluded to the killer instinct and how important it was to compete well. When I approached the prerace favorite, I proceeded to shock him by saying, "I hope you have a great race." Confused by the words, the favorite inquired as to why I felt that way. I told him, "The better you run, the better I will, too." The favorite did win the race and I claimed third, running my fastest time for the distance—and, in the process, pushing the winner to one of his greatest victories.

Another national champion runner was in the middle of her race, feeling as if she were doing the best she could do. At that moment, two opponents came from behind and began to pass her. Her first reaction was to quit; they were too strong and she couldn't keep up. But, remembering the meaning of true competition, she asked herself perhaps the most important question one can ask in the midst of an all-out race: *What can I do now? Now that I'm tired, now that I'm getting dropped, now that I'm losing confidence.* By focusing on what you can do as opposed to what you can't, you begin to take positive action, digging down deep inside to discover what is there rather than what's not. She decided not to let them take off without her, and committed to stay with them for the next 50 meters. In the process of that small, manageable distance, she discovered reservoirs of strength and energy she had not known she had and regained her lead before the final straightaway; she went on to win the race. Her opponents gave her an opportunity to see what she had left; they were gifts in disguise. Even had she not held up, she would have given all that she could by accepting the challenge posed by her competitors.

Embrace Your Competitor

Here is a mind shift to practice in your next race; embrace competitors as partners who, because of their outstanding performance, help you to understand yourself more fully to bring out your best. Begin to experience the powerful advantages of working together; synergistic competition provides a surplus of energy for positive performance. Try this experiment: in your next race, talk out loud to your competitors all along the race. This works especially well when you are on a familiar home course. Say things like *Big uphill ahead; Steep downhill around the bend; Loose gravel cresting the hill.* You will find that these words of encouragement for others will also keep your spirits and energy high.

There is a Chinese parable that describes the difference between heaven and hell. Each place is an enormous banquet with delectable foods. All are given five-foot-long chopsticks. In the banquet in hell, people struggle to manipulate these awkward utensils and give up out of frustration and starve. In heaven, everyone serves the person across the table and each becomes abundantly full.

In the banquet of competitive running, you want an opponent who will feed you his best challenge, a clean, true surge that awaits your full response. With this great gift each runner rises to the top, each "feeding" the other delicious morsels of competitive spirit as each becomes filled with true greatness. Let others be your spiritual running advisors who facilitate your growth as an athlete. See the advantage of having your opponents around; don't seek to "kill" them off. By so doing, you may perform at higher levels more consistently.

With this attitude shift, you have the fullness of healthy competition, a mutually shared running and racing experience, one where you feel more alive from having "died" as a result of each of you pushing the boundaries of your full potential. It is a profound and rare occurrence where you witness the potential of all who choose to enter this arena, this community of competitive runners who all ultimately reach the winner's podium.

Perhaps we need to view our runs, racing, or any competitive situation in life as a contest. The Latin word for contest is *contestari*, meaning "to call to witness." Your opponents are witnesses to what you do; in every race you take a pledge to do your best. You give your word to be a good competitor and thank the opposition for keeping you honest. In turn, you offer them the opportunity to take the same pledge. You are both there to teach each other how to be your best. To help you focus on this more productive mind-set, we offer you the following visualization and affirmations.

Visualization

In your deeply relaxed state, close your eyes and visualize the following to become more competitive in this new way.

Imagine coming face to face with an opponent.

Feel the energy of this person who is willing to give his or her best.

Notice your opponent's pleasure in knowing you will provide the same.

As the competition begins, feel the exhilaration of the challenge.

Imagine how each of you gives your best, back and forth, throughout the race.

Feel the mutual appreciation you have for each other when the race is completed.

Affirmations

Use these while visualizing, and create some of your own in the blanks. Recite them often.

I embrace my opponent as an opportunity for me to perform well.

Working together, we achieve so much more.

Competition is the key to fruition.

My opponent is a gift who pushes me to greater heights.

_____

_____

_____

_____

chapter 8

Winning as a Journey

In his classic work *The Zen of Running*, Fred Rohé eloquently states, "There are no victories except the joy you are living while dancing your run; you are not running for some future reward— the real reward is *now!*" The modern Olympic games motto, *The goal is not to win, but to take part,* tells us that the essence of the race is not conquering but competing well. Both of these statements parallel the credo of *Running Within,* which embraces victory as a path without a destination and reminds us that, as stated by Cervantes' Don Quixote, the journey is better than the inn.

As runners, we can all remember the times when we were winners, even if the race results didn't acknowledge it. I (Jerry) finished 143rd out of 310 runners at the Stanford Invitational cross-country race. By most participants' standards, this was not considered a winning performance. For me, however, it was a major victory because I ran my fastest time for the distance and did it against some of the best collegiate athletes in the United States, all of whom were 20 or more years younger than I. It was an inner, personal triumph, one most could not see. When the process itself is fulfilling and you win in the moment, victory is always the experience; external results are ephemeral, while internal victories last a lifetime.

Many runners, focused solely on PRs, place, time, and ranking, lose sight of their journey and suffocate the joy of running by overemphasizing the importance of these outcomes. This preoccupation with the traditional extrinsic definition of winning, at its worst, can lead athletes to blood doping and illegal drugs such as anabolic steroids. These alleged performance-enhancing aids may result in a slight advantage for awhile, but they eventually lead to the athlete's demise. Researcher and writer Gabe Mirkin polled over 100 runners on whether they would consider swallowing a pill that would make them an Olympic champion, yet kill them in a year. Fifty percent said they would take the pill. What a price to pay for gold. At best, our distraction over extrinsic winning creates enormous pressure, anxiety, and tension, making it difficult to focus on the task of running well; we empty our physiological reserves to fill our egos. It is a no-win situation.

Let Go of the Need to Win and Be Victorious

Many of us have heard of the scholar Joseph Campbell, but few know about Joseph the runner. Back in the 1920s, he was a world-class half-miler running for Columbia's track team. In one of the few races he ever lost, he claimed that he was defeated because winning was too important to him. He was thrown off because he showed up with a deep need to win the race rather than to run the race—run it like the champion he was. The focus on needing to win created debilitating anxiety and tension that interfered with his performance.

Speed skating world champion Dan Jansen also has had the "Campbell experience." Missing the gold in the 500-meter race at three consecutive Olympiads, he and his coach decided that he should show up and simply *race* the 1000-meter event. Relaxed, calm, and fluid, with no expectations to win, Dan went on to capture the gold in this race, setting an Olympic record in the process. Although Dan is not a runner, the concept of letting go of the need to win and the anxiety that need creates applies to all runners—and all athletes—who ever entertain the thought of victory. We must define what victory means for each of us individually, and then proceed to measure our success by how close we come to it. In the process, winning on the scoreboard becomes much more likely. Let go of the need to win, and victory—that is, experiencing personal victory—will be yours.

This isn't to say that winning—crossing the finish line first, recording a personal best time, and so on—is unimportant. There's a huge difference, however, between needing to win and wanting to win. *Needing* is tied into self-worth; many need to win in order to feel okay, not only as runners but also as people. For them, not winning means losing, and this becomes a commentary about who they are. The runner who experiences running within, on the other hand, *wants* victory—it's fun and joyous when you have a goal to win and then strategically execute the plan to perfection. Even if you fall short of the plan, you are able to see the goal of winning simply as a challenge worth striving for, a lantern that illuminates your way on the path of excellence and becoming your best.

The key to shifting your mind toward running within is to not detach from winning; instead, detach your ego from winning. Enjoy the process of the run every step of the way. This is a victory. Have fun running with good form and smooth strides. This is a win. Run your very best, feeling healthy and strong. This is a triumph. When you invest your self-esteem in the outcome of an event, you give that event power over your life—to make you happy, to make you sad, to place you in an emotional whirlwind. Such an investment will only deplete your energy, create anxiety, and slow you down.

Winning, therefore, becomes an exhilarating journey without a finish line. When you create this shift in consciousness, the by-product is usually external victory—whether it is finishing the race, winning your age group, setting a personal best, or finishing in the top 20 percent.

Control What You Can

Any attempt to control the results or outcome of a run or race is useless. Trying to control that which cannot be controlled creates the usual counterproductive physiological reactions of anxiety, pressure, and tension.

To not control what can be controlled results in tremendous disappointment and regret. You can control how you choose to run—your pace, your form, your surges, and your training program. Focusing on these aspects of a run or race is to exert your presence and influence how the event unfolds.

Olympian and world silver medalist Regina Jacobs was about to run the 1500-meter national championships in Knoxville, Tennessee. Knowing she was coming up against a deep field of talented women, she expressed concern over how to beat her competitors and win the race. She learned to relax physiologically by not trying to control the outcome and instead focusing on her plan, something she could control. She used an affirmation as a reminder—a touchstone—during the moments when self-doubt would creep in, and this relaxed her even further. On an index card, she wrote, *I may or may not win, but I run like an incredible national champion.* She then defined what that meant and visualized running that way. She ran like a champion—relaxed,

smooth, fluid, strong—and as a result, won the national title. According to Regina, the race was quite easy. She was pleasantly surprised at how little physical effort it required; she simply exerted her influence and controlled what she could.

Guides to Letting Go

Racing is a process, the outcome of which simply measures how successful you have been moment by moment throughout the event as well as your training and preparation. Success in the *now* is a factor of the joy you experience in the execution of a plan, the quality demonstrated in your technique and skill level. When you acknowledge that winning is beyond your control, you can begin to fully experience the emotional rush of competition: well-trained athletes seeking greatness together. Seeing the race as a journey, you feel the freedom to run in the flow, a state of relaxed intensity. Here are some specific strategies to help you let go of those things you can't control by focusing on those things that you can control.

Form Focus

To stay in the moment, focus on your cadence, your form, your pace, and your stride. And remember this: there is no victory other than the joy you experience when "dancing" on the terrain. The real treasure is *now*.

You have trained for many hours, so your body knows what to do. You just need to let your mind be in harmony with your knowledgeable body and not stand in its way by being hypercritical and obsessed with winning. A fixed, rigid mind creates a fixed, rigid body. When you trust in your body and resist the obsession with outcomes, you create a free-flowing mind and a free-flowing body in a mutually satisfying partnership of body, mind, and spirit. When a well-trained racehorse enters the starting gate, it doesn't look around and analyze the competition. It simply waits for the gate to open, and at the bell it lets the body do its thing— to simply run the race. The stallion loves the process and never once thinks about the finish. Like the racehorse, show up and turn your mind over to your body as you enjoy the process.

Clear Confidence

Hold on to the notion of *real confidence*. Many runners say that they have lost confidence in winning; how can you have confidence in doing something that you can't control such as winning? Once you realize the futility in striving for the impossible, you can then discover the confidence you can experience, not in an outcome, but in the decisions you make during the run or race. Know that you may or may not win, but you can have confidence in running like a winner—which, paradoxically, gives you more control over the outcome. Have confidence in your ability to run and race as you do in training in the absence of performance anxiety, where there is nothing at stake.

Get the Job Done

Just do it; race without care. Dan Jansen finally won the gold when he decided not to care so much. As a competitive group, runners are too concerned about doing it right. We need to try to enter one race and not give a damn; when we do, we will be better able to relax and run. Sometimes it's more fun to show up and say *To hell with it,* "it" being the outcome. Having acknowledged that, proceed to race with what we call *effortless effort,* an attitude of asserting your level of fitness (showing what you've got) without the conscious attempt to do well.

Visualize Your Race

It's important to know that in your mental race preparation it's healthy to visualize winning (against the clock, against an opponent, or for a certain place in the finish), but not to the exclusion of seeing the process unfold as it should. However, when you actually show up at the event, do so to simply run your best for that day. Remember that wanting to win and needing to win are very different attitudes toward racing. The former is healthy; the latter is destructive.

Visualization

In your deeply relaxed state, close your eyes and visualize the following to be victorious.

Imagine pushing yourself to run the best you can.

Feel the confidence from performing as you know you can.

Sense the moment-to-moment thrill and excellence.

Experience the fun as you execute your well-defined plan.

Feel the joy, the dance, and the flow of running a great race.

Affirmations

Use these while visualizing. Create your own in the blanks, and recite them often.

I am a winner, regardless of the outcome.

Winning is a journey without a destination.

I focus on the process, and the results take care of themselves.

I can't control the outcome, but I take charge of how I run.

I may or may not win, but I run like a well-trained athlete.

The real reward is now!

Let go and go with the flow.

_____

_____

_____

_____

III

Performing With Intent

Now that you are fortified with positive mental shifts in attitude toward winning, losing, and competing, and you are experiencing running differently, you are ready to direct your attention toward performing with the intent, the driving force, the will, underlying the action. You may want to go back to chapter 1 on motivation and goals for a quick review. In this part of the running-within journey, you will learn to stoke your passion and discover the fun of the run with the gain-without-strain approach to training. All of you who intend to compete will become more racewise when you develop your mental best, for training as well as for pre-, post- and during the event (chapter 9). To perform optimally, you will need to examine any rigid beliefs you may have about what's possible and take the steps to transcend these limits (chapter 10). Once you do, you will be ready to get into your flow and focus with determination as you carry through with your plan to full completion. Here you will find the way to concentrate on the pure spirit of running, a special place where you can have the opportunity to use new shifts in consciousness to cultivate deeper intention with your racing performance (chapter 11). Without intention, nothing gets accomplished. With it, magic happens. What you intend will portend—a foreshadowing of what will be.

chapter 9

Preparing for Race Day

W hat part of race performance can be attributed to mental strength? According to legendary coach Bud Winter from San Jose State, "When all your skills have been honed to razor sharpness and when your physical condition is at its zenith, then the difference between winning and losing is generally mental."

What are some of the more popular concerns runners have with respect to mental and emotional race preparation? Most runners have questions about levels of arousal, maintaining concentration and confidence, coping mentally with tactical errors (going out too fast, for example), fatigue, opposition, unexpected occurrences (weather changes, crowds, hills), and pain. Some runners even express interest in learning how to cope better with postrace feelings of disappointment, anger, or frustration over their failure to perform up to expectations. Each of these concerns fits into one of three categories: prerace, during race, and postrace. This chapter touches on these psychophysiological needs to get you ready for the big day. Although we can't possibly cover every concern of each athlete, there is enough laterality to enable you to improvise and adapt these strategies to your individual needs.

When do you start preparing for a race? Some runners, like Olympian Lee Evans, have prepared their minds for years preceding the one big event. Others feel that two to three months will do it. There's no such thing as too soon; the more crucial the race, the earlier you should begin your mental preparation. However, a good rule of thumb for most races is to begin two to four weeks prior to the event. Sometimes athletes will train mentally for only two to three days the week of the race, particularly if they are mentally fit and simply need fine-tuning. For the purposes of this chapter, we'll simulate a typical mental training program broken into three segments: two weeks before competition, during competition, and the postrace period.

Remember that from a physiological perspective, the race-ready runner is well rested, tapered, maximally hydrated, and carboloaded. Prerace tapering includes reducing training volume significantly to about 25 to 35 percent of your weekly routine.

Prerace Strategies

Your primary objective during the two weeks (at least) prior to your race is to build confidence by drawing from past successes

and by visually rehearsing the upcoming event in its entirety; anticipating the unexpected and reacting favorably to such occurrences is part of this visual imagery rehearsal. Your basic tools for achieving those tasks, the same as they have been all along the journey, are relaxation, visualization, and affirmation. Apply these principles as discussed in part I. The following guidelines are meant to give direction, but feel free to experiment and create your own scenarios. You are limited only by your imagination.

Visualize Your Workouts

All workouts should be preceded by 10 to 15 minutes of relaxation, visualization, and affirmations in order for you to master the body–mind–spirit journey. Since you race as you train, be sure to rehearse visual images in your training runs each day. Feel yourself surge with the ease of a graceful cat. Imagine the nutrients flowing to your muscles as you feel fantastic gliding across the terrain. Being in a relaxed state prior to a workout allows the body to run more fluidly and improves the circulation of the blood with its vital supply of oxygen.

Study the Course

You can benefit from knowing the course in advance. If it's local, drive or bike it in both directions, and even run various sections. If this is not possible, get a description from someone who has run the course; often, race directors will provide the information upon request.

Knowing what lies ahead will build confidence before as well as during a race. Surprises cause anxiety, which takes a toll on confidence. Eliminating the unknown is a distinct advantage for optimal performance. For example, an athlete was running a marathon, a brutal course winding up and over the Santa Cruz Mountains. The illusion that most runners had after 11 miles of uphill running was that the remaining part of the race was gravy, and they would be able to coast down to the finish. Much to their chagrin, they were greeted by a series of four long, challenging, rolling inclines at mile 22—and, as if to add insult to injury, the finish chute was perched at the top of a 300-yard rising grade. Fortunately for this runner, he had run that final 4-mile stretch a half-dozen times prior to the race, and planned his strategy with those undulations in mind; he visualized himself gliding up the hills and finishing strong. He was not to be denied that day as he squeaked out a narrow victory ahead of some talented runners who were on unfamiliar ground.

The neurophysiology of this occurrence is based in the limbic system. Familiar territory is calming. Unfamiliar territory is arousing, stressful, and unpredictable. In this case, the familiarity with the difficult course yielded a relaxing and powerful response. You can observe your heart rate, breathing, muscle tension, and perceived effort over familiar and unfamiliar race courses to see the truth in this physiological phenomenon.

A positive experience on a familiar course can help you prepare for your future races both on that course and on different courses as well by capturing those positive feelings of fluidity, effortlessness, and strength. In some cases you won't have the advantage of seeing the course you will run ahead of time, but you can still mentally prepare for the challenges of such a course. In a relaxed state, you want to visualize how you felt during previous successful performances. Get in touch with those memories and transfer them to the upcoming event and the course you'll be running. Recall how quickly and smoothly you ran, how you glided past others, how you surged throughout and floated across the finish line in a personal best. Remember, that was you and it can be repeated.

If you had a bad experience the last time you ran on a particular course, you can turn this into a challenge and positive experience. Reframe the negative experience as an opportunity that can teach you how to become a better runner. Rerun in your mind those negative parts of the race in a way that would make you feel successful.

Rehearsing Your Prerace Routine

We strongly urge you to begin your rehearsal by "seeing" yourself one hour before the race. Is there grass around you? How does it feel, smell? How do you look as you warm up and jog to the starting line? Feel composed, poised, and confident, ready to burst forward like a contained horse let loose. Pay close attention to your body. As your rehearsals become more complete, you may notice an increase in heart rate or breathing rate. You may begin to sweat and feel tension in your belly. These are normal physiological changes that accompany your mental training drills. As you rehearse the race, get in touch with how it feels to run your best, and imagine the race unfolding exactly as you would like. Carry your visualization through the award ceremony (if that's in your plan) and into the evening. See yourself enjoying the fact that you performed well earlier in the day; imagine what it would be like to eat your favorite meal with close friends discussing the race. Don't leave anything out. Rehearsal should encompass every aspect of the entire day.

Simulation Training

How can you rehearse all aspects of the race when the unexpected usually happens? Running the Boston Marathon, for example, can mean the possibility of being exposed to numerous unpredictable weather conditions. You rehearsed the perfect race, except you forgot to do it in the driving wind and rain. Unless you plan to run in San Diego or Phoenix, the probability of climate changes is a reality to contend with.

Other changes and unexpected scenarios may conflict with your rehearsal. Perhaps there are many more people in the race than expected, or your nemesis decides to show; both situations could ruin your plans. Therefore, it is crucial that you include in your visualization of the event all the extraneous possibilities that come to mind in what is called *simulation training*. Some situations, obviously, will remain unpredictable. It's impossible to cover all eventualities.

Like physical simulation, the mind needs to be trained to respond favorably in case you're exposed to something not planned for. The key is to think of all the negative possibilities (don't plan on snow or cold if the probability is minimal), include them in a few of your rehearsal sessions, and "see" yourself responding to the unexpected in a positive, effective manner. Simulate possible mistakes made while racing, and imagine how you would recover from them successfully if they actually occurred. Think of these race situations over and over. As you rehearse them in your mind, pay close attention to your heart rate and breathing. Review the list of potential race problems and observe which scenarios produce nervousness and anxiety, manifested as sweaty palms and butterflies in your stomach. Use these physiological cues as signs that you need to mentally prepare for these potential anxiety-producing situations. The final outcome should be a calm, relaxed, strong, energy-efficient athlete.

Ritualize

The more familiar your routine just prior to an event is, the more control you have over anxiety. Ritual is a habit requiring little or no thought; subsequently, it is relaxing, reducing tension and fear over the possibility of forgetting something at the last minute (dietary, equipment, and travel concerns are a few). Aside from this, the ritual becomes a familiar stimulus that serves to remind you of the upcoming event. It is learned over time by repeating the same format before each race. For example, when you begin to carboload before a marathon, you know the race is three days away; when you climb into your racing shoes, it's now posttime—here comes the adrenaline. Such a training mechanism takes the place of thinking, *The race is about to begin; am I ready?* The simple act of putting on the shoes will stimulate the appropriate emotions.

Everything you do in the last 48 hours before a race is part of a ritual. It gives you confidence because it's something familiar—you've been there before. Such behavior explains why some athletes will wear the same singlet or shorts. If they raced well with these garments once, many will try to wear them to every race. Such behavior is acceptable if you are flexible with it. Just as you need to visualize and prepare for changes in weather, you need to visualize running perhaps in a different shirt or socks, in case something prevents you from wearing your preferred garments. Remember that the best athletes are flexible and adaptive.

Some runners ritualize with a movie—nothing too heavy or draining—two nights before the race. This can divert attention from the event and help to improve sleep. Dinner is also part of the routine. The night before the race, eat the same food that has worked well in the past. If you're on the road, take familiar food along in case it's not available. On race morning, you don't want any surprises or extra trips to the porta-toilet.

Another helpful ritual is having a checklist of all that needs to be done prior to race day: arrange for travel; set the alarm to help you wake up (two alarms if you want to be extra sure); fill the gas tank the night before if you're driving to a race; gather clothing to be worn pre-, during, and postrace; pin a race number to your singlet; pack Vaseline, water, and racing shoes. You might even want to develop a personalized packing list that you use to check off all things that are important for you to remember. Not worrying about these items right before your race allows you to concentrate on the event itself.

The key to making rituals work is consistency. No matter what routine you establish, be sure it's a consistent, bit-by-bit pursuit. By so doing, you will begin to experience a more consistent optimal level of performance. If something that worked for you in the past no longer feels good, try something new. Don't be consistent simply for consistency's sake. Foolish consistency is the hobgoblin of little minds. Always welcome a change in the routine if there's a chance it will help.

Set Multiple Goals

As discussed in chapter 1, be sure you've set two or three realistic but challenging goals, and include a range. For example, if running a marathon, select a range within which you would like to finish. Perhaps you could choose a finish between 2:58 and 3:15. This is more relaxing than expecting to hit one magical number. You will then go into the race confident and more relaxed, knowing that the outcome will be positive and that you are likely to achieve one or two good results. Other goals you might set for yourself include running negative splits or even-paced miles, finishing at a certain percentile of all entrants, or completing the run injury free.

Race Strategies

The moment has arrived. It is time to put it all together; you have planned the work, now work the plan. Your training is complete, and you are as ready as can be. Show up to run, have fun, and set your body free to do all it was trained to do. Take a few minutes to reflect and meditate on how fit and ready you are and how fortunate you feel to be in good health and able to participate in the race. Experience the joy, sense your pride, and congratulate yourself on achieving the benefits of your training program. That, in itself, is a victory worth celebrating.

Remind yourself that your mission is simply to race the best you can and not obsess about the outcome. Focus on running one mile at a time. Think *soft is strong*—this reminds you to run fluidly and not force or push. Run smarter, not harder, by thinking calm and tranquil thoughts. Meditative states create extraordinary performance.

In an ideal situation, the event will require little mental energy other than steady concentration, and your body will react instinctively to the demands placed on it. However, this ideal situation rarely happens. More than likely, you will need to respond to a myriad of emotionally charged circumstances that will test the outer boundaries of your mental stamina. Try to predict your splits throughout the race, and maintain an even pace over the entire distance, except for the final kick. From a physiological point of view, this proves to be the most economical method of racing. Distractions and negative thoughts filter into your cognitive being, sending distress signals to the body. Fear of slowing to a snail's pace, being passed by other competitors, or possibly not finishing the race create unwanted anxiety and tension. Then, of course, there are the elements of fatigue and pain, old friends that would love to come along for the ride. Some situations will be entirely familiar; you may even have planned for them. Others will be totally unexpected. In any event, your work will be cut out for you. The following represent the more recurrent areas of concern that athletes have brought to our attention, and strategies to help ameliorate them.

Dealing With Distractions

Pain could be a positive distraction—your body's way of signaling distress—and deserves your attention. If you determine that a pain is not serious, then the distraction should be shelved. For example, the onset of a stitch is a physical distraction, but its effect will be minimized if you concentrate on the rhythm of your breathing or the cadence of your stride. Perhaps your distraction is mental; you wish the race were over or you're worried about a work-related problem. Remember that any distraction will persist if you resist. Rather than expending energy fighting the distraction, view it as a friend who visits occasionally. Give it credence by talking to it: *Hi, it's you again; well, I'm busy right now, so how about talking later?* This will give you greater control over any anxiety that may arise from the distraction. Taming such distractions helps you to reduce muscle tension, allowing for easier breathing, which ultimately improves your running economy. Choose to view distractions as a challenge or an opportunity to practice concentration while on the run.

Keeping Your Focus

Many runners' mental breaking points are tested when the outcome of the race looks dismal: fears of slowing, not finishing, or being passed in the late stages are demoralizing. The brain sends messages to throw in the towel with phrases such as *Let them go, it's not important; I'd rather be at that picnic; Who needs this?* or, *It's too much farther to continue.* Whether you are an elite or recreational athlete, the fears and anxieties are similar.

The first step in dealing with this crisis is to focus on what can be done now. Don't think about the future (the rest of the race, tomorrow, or the day after). If the grandfather clock knew how many times it had to tick in its lifetime, it would have given up long ago. Divide the task into small, manageable segments. When a runner goes by, one who looks fairly strong and fresh and is running a bit faster than you, strive to hang on—not necessarily until the end of the race (or at least tell yourself that)—but for a specific distance or time such as 1 mile, 6 minutes, or whatever is comfortable. At that segment, focus on your feelings. At the very worst, you will have run better for that distance than if you had given up. At best, you may catch a second wind and run one of your best races. By telling yourself that you only need to follow that runner for a short distance, the task won't seem as psychologically overwhelming.

Shorten the distance of any race by running each mile one at a time. For example, when Soren, a 64-year-old ultradistance runner, reached the finish line of the Western States 100-miler, a reporter asked him how someone his age runs 100 miles. Soren replied, "I don't run 100 miles; I run 1 mile 100 times." By focusing on one mile at a time, Soren can go the distance. If he focused on the whole distance, the mere thought of such a task would distract and fatigue him.

Detaching Yourself From the Outcome

By detaching yourself from the outcome during a race and letting go of anxiety over performance, you'll become more relaxed and find energy you didn't know you had. Focus, instead, on the fun, the exhilaration of simply running a well-executed plan. Concentrate on how much you love running and how fortunate you are to be healthy and strong enough to run this race.

Don't cease to care about the outcome of your race, but detach from measuring your self-worth as a runner based on whether you reach all of your goals. Reaching all of one's goals is a measure of many things, but not of your self-worth. You are a well-trained athlete regardless of the outcome. Basically, goal realization is an

© Beth Schneider

indicator that you are on the path to improvement. Remember, however, that the goals are beacons that keep you going forward in the process. Successful processes usually result in successful outcomes. When you let go, you'll gain the freedom to run the race completely uninhibited, the way it was meant to be.

Postrace Strategies

A complete program for mental race preparation should take into account your feelings and concerns following the event as well as those prior to and during. Managing postevent tensions, anxieties, frustrations, and disappointments is vital for performance in future competitive efforts. As we discussed in chapter 6, your running log might be of help if you record these responses in order to gain some insight into your racing. Take time out to examine the meaning of a win or loss; put into proper perspective, you can gain a lot of information from such analysis. For example, you might not have come in first, yet your performance was a personal best; besides, you might have learned some valuable strategies for future competition as a result of not coming in first. Cautiously interpret the outcome as a success or failure: a loss is not necessarily an unsuccessful effort. In our experience, most successful runners wait until the day after their event to objectively criticize and assess the outcome.

We want to stress the importance of taking "alone time" to rehash your thoughts; do this on a slow, gentle run, or take 15 minutes to relax and ask yourself, *What have I learned from this experience that will help me to develop my potential? Did I go out too fast? Did I neglect to stop at enough aid stations and become dehydrated? Did I surge too often? Do I need to do more long runs in training?* Apply whatever you come up with to your future strategies.

We also strongly suggest talking these feelings out with someone you know who understands the situation. You'll discover that others experience similar feelings of discontent, and this will help release anxiety and tension. Following a poor race that I (Jerry) did not finish, I decided to call some running buddies to discuss the circumstances. The consensus was that everyone who races eventually will post a DNF (did not finish). I was able to forgive myself more quickly because I knew that I was in good company.

Performance on any level requires an athlete to deal with the psychological as well as the physical. To overlook this is to leave the outcome to luck or chance. Such uncertainty is unnecessary; you can gain greater control over your racing by experimenting with the various mental strategies and techniques just discussed. You will begin to take charge of your performance and optimize the chances of success when you race with your head as well as your body. Sharpen your mental game plan and begin to enjoy the benefits a trained mind can bring to your sport.

Visualization

In a deeply relaxed state, close your eyes and visualize the following. There are many variations of visualizing for your race; think about your personal goals and concerns and develop your own for each circumstance.

See yourself at the race, warming up and stretching.

Watch all the runners as they go through their routines.

Feel the excitement and adrenaline, familiar sensations prior to a race.

You begin the race feeling relaxed, strong, and fluid.

Feel the force of a headwind pushing you back, and see how you easily adapt to this obstacle by becoming a wedge and slicing through it with ease.

Here comes a hill; feel yourself glide over it effortlessly.

The race is over and you have accomplished much. Feel successful.

Feel exhilarated by the results, as you taste the sweetness of orange wedges.

Affirmations

Use these during your visualization, create a few of your own in the blanks, and be sure to recite them daily.

Calm and confident, I race well.

Expect success, I'm running my best.

Every race is a new opportunity to improve my skills.

I possess all that I need to race like a well-trained athlete.

_____

_____

_____

_____

Examining and Transcending Limits

Keith Foreman, an accomplished Masters-level runner, attended the Big Lake Running Camp in the mountains of Oregon. He was like a sponge, soaking up all the cutting-edge information about running psychology and physiology he could. On one of his daily exploration runs along the Pacific Crest Trail, we talked about how beliefs are, indeed, limits that stand in the way. Having said this, we proceeded to have an unbelievable run on terrain that seemed impossible to traverse. While dancing up a 15 percent grade, speaking four words per breath, Keith told a story about his running experiences while attending the University of Oregon in the early 1960s.

Keith had a deep desire to be part of the track team. The Oregon Ducks were loaded with talent that year, and the head coach told Keith that his chances for making the squad were minimal. Naturally, no scholarships would be available. With an open mind and heart, Keith gave it a shot, believing that with a deep commitment to diligent work, he might be able to fit in. And fit in he did, as he became the fifth American ever to break 4 minutes in the mile. Keith refused to believe the limits placed upon him by his coach, and is now regarded as one of the university's greatest athletes of all time.

Keith exhibited a trait that is universal among all successful people: they have no fixed minds; they are flexible and open in their beliefs. Fixed mind-sets about what is possible obscure the unlimited boundaries of your potential. Rigid, fixed minds also make for rigid bodies and tight, inflexible running performances. Elite athletes, as well as all of us ready to move to higher levels of performance, see all beliefs as unnecessary limitations to be examined, scrutinized, and challenged.

I Can

Henry Ford, a man who knew a thing or two about movement, once proclaimed, "Whether you think you can or think you can't, you're probably right." Believing you can't forces you to sabotage any efforts that you might make to accomplish a goal. For example, if you actually believe you can't break 3 hours in the marathon, why would you try to seek out ways to help you accomplish what you believe to be impossible? Believe you can, and you will activate all the psychological processes—courage, commitment, motivation, confidence, and excitement—that will place you on the path of attainment. You begin to search for ways to make your dream a reality, bringing your goal to fruition. As long as you say *I can,* you will feel alive and begin to unlock the extraordinary potential you possess. To believe otherwise prevents you from even trying. After Bannister broke 4 minutes, dozens of other athletes decided that they could too—and within 18 months did so.

As a body–mind–spirit runner, you need to consistently fight your tendency to think and believe restrictively about what is possible; you have unlimited potential as a runner once you are able to say *I can.* By acting as if you can accomplish something, you create the process of self-direction, not self-deception. Such a stance puts you on the road of excellence in all that you do, if you are willing to learn from setbacks, make proper adjustments, and forge ahead. Elite runners and champions in all sports excel because they are free of mind-sets that obscure the unlimited boundaries of their potential. They have opened themselves up to all possibilities, say *I can,* and seek ways to explore their potential.

Olympian Wilma Rudolph had polio as a child; doctors told her that she had little chance of ever walking again without leg braces. In and out of hospitals for many of her early years, she refused to believe these experts, choosing instead to defeat this crippling disease using the *I can* philosophy. And that she did on her way to winning three Olympic gold medals. Like Wilma, you are capable of extraordinary things when you affirm *I can* and apply yourself accordingly.

Acting As If

We are taught to neutralize any force with its opposite: fight fire with water, anger with love. And runners need to fight *I can't* with *I can.* When we do, we can alter our performance reality. Beginning to believe *I can* rather than *I can't* is facilitated by adopting the *act as if* mind-set. Simply act as if you can.

Ask a good runner, someone you respect, for some good training tips that support your goals and objectives. Ask about lifestyle changes and other variables that contribute to excellence in performance. Notice how these athletes race, and mimic them. Find out how champions do it, and imitate them in all possible ways, given your own limitations at this time. Do all that you think is necessary to be that champion. Act as if you are an accomplished athlete, and you will do the things necessary to keep you on track.

While working with elite runners and cyclists, we have had the opportunity to work out with those we respect. We run and ride with these accomplished athletes, trying to learn all that we can by imitating their technique and style. By acting as if we were these athletes in future workouts, our performance level rises a few notches. We try to imitate models of excellence in all aspects of our sport for racing and all of life. We act as if we can, and we do. Realize that these elite athletes are people, just like you. They too had mentors or teachers early in their training whom they could imitate to improve their levels of performance.

Now think about a challenge you would like to take on as a runner, but believe you can't take on. List all the reasons why you believe you can't. How valid are these reasons? What if you acted as if you could, then approached your obstacle or challenge and gave it a try? For example, you may believe you can't finish a marathon under 3:30. Why do you believe this? What if you were able to do all that was necessary to accomplish this and proceeded to act as if you could do it? You must refrain from judging or criticizing yourself and assume that the challenge is possible unless the data you collect conclusively proves you wrong.

As you begin to take on this obstacle, you may discover from closer range ways that are available to help you surmount the hurdle. For example, you may want to climb a 15-foot brick wall, but from a distance it looks impossible. If you approach it, you may notice openings and protruding bricks, which give your feet and hands the chance to step up and hold on as you gingerly crawl to the top. Do the same with your running objectives. Collect the data. Notice that you can be successful in your task if you refuse to believe anything other than it can be done. Proceed by acting as if by approaching and seeing it at close range that it is possible. Too often we determine the feasibility of performing a task before we collect the important data and develop a plan to meet the task.

When we work with athletes who want to believe that a particular task is within grasp, we encourage them to restrain from comments such as *I'm not good enough; I can't do it; I'm too old, fat, slow; I'm not ready; I don't deserve . . . ;* and follow this four-step exercise.

© Terry Wild

1. **Don't make a judgment about what you can and can't do until the data are in.** Decide what you'd like to do (what your goals are) and go for it! Go up to your wall, take a good look, and search for ways to hurdle it one brick at a time. When I (Jerry) thought I was too old, too heavy, and too slow to run competitively, I took on the challenge of racing. When I began at the age of 34, I could barely run a mile without stopping—but with a productive training program, I became a regional and national champion by the age of 42. Naturally, this took me several years, but my goals served as beacons to keep me on track. There was some trial and error; but overall, with patience and perseverance, my training paid off because I always acted as if I could do it. This plus proper dietary fuel and rest enabled me to develop as a national-class runner.

2.   **Make believe.** Act as if you're going to reach your goal. You have to see it in your mind to believe it. Use imagery and visualization. Imagine yourself running your special race, running fast and under control; see the course, hear the sounds, see the finish line clock showing your PR. See yourself sharing your accomplishment with family and friends. Imagine writing your new PR in your logbook.

Anderson University's cross-country team in Indiana follows the act-as-if formula that we talked about, going so far as printing the slogan *Act as if* on school T-shirts. Acting as if they are champions, they have produced several All-American distance stars.

3.   **Don't think hate, think love.** Use this as a basis for affirmations. If you think you hate hills, you'll never run them successfully. As we discussed in chapter 7, hate thoughts physiologically slow you down. For some, such negative emotions as hate and anger seem to work; but eventually these athletes would probably perform better if their nervous systems were bathed in positive thought patterns. Strong negative emotional thoughts induce limbic excitation, which in turn tenses your muscles and increases your heart rate, blood pressure, and energy utilization, yielding suboptimal running. When you affirm that you love hills, you'll enjoy attacking them and feel invigorated as you run them with good form. You can make hill running one of your strengths when you learn to love them because they help train your heart and lungs in a way that no other workout can. Love the fact that they create opportunities for you to become a better athlete.

4.   **Think about all the times in the past when you couldn't quite believe that your present level of fitness and running would eventually be possible.** Use those instances as reference points to remind yourself that your present limited beliefs are no different than those you had in the past; those changed and so will these. Trust . . . and believe it. You might want to review your logbook to see what you have accomplished and how you did it; review the steps you took in the process.

To develop strong beliefs in yourself as a runner, construct a number of affirmations that make firm what you must believe to achieve. For example, if you are in position to make the Olympic team, affirm, *I am a member of the U.S. Olympic team.* Perhaps your ambition is to be one of the top runners in your age group regionally or locally; affirm that you are. Maybe you'd like to finish consistently in the top 10 in all of your races or simply run well in each event; affirm this too. Remember from part I that affirmations are a way for you to be self-directive, not self-deceptive. Self-direction helps you to act as if your dream is true. The key to realistic, effective affirmations is to wisely assess your potential, then stretch a bit, reaching beyond your present position and affirming that place as if it were true.

Finally, keep in mind that a lack of belief in your ability to perform is your opponent's greatest advantage. Now begin to take the aforementioned steps to reinforce strong attitudes about your performance on the path to becoming the best runner you can be. You have the choice to view your competitive potential in a more constructive, positive fashion. To get beyond your limitations, keep your mind wide open and begin to release old, worn-out beliefs; give yourself permission to discard attitudes that pose as obstacles and are no longer applicable or appropriate for you on your path of success as a runner.

We have seen thousands of runners over the years who, by changing their long-held narrow beliefs, have changed the outcomes of their performances. What you believe, you will achieve.

Visualization

In a deeply relaxed state, close your eyes and visualize the following to help yourself believe you can and act as if.

Think of a situation where your belief is an obstacle: *I can't; I'm too old.*

See yourself performing as if you are able to do it with skill and dexterity.

Feel in the groove, running like the natural athlete you are.

Feel confident as you steadily progress and improve as an accomplished runner.

Feel ecstatic about being capable of challenging your belief and going beyond it.

Affirmations

Use these during your visualization, create a few of your own in the blanks, and be sure to recite them daily.

If I shoot for the sun and miss, I'll become one of the stars.

When I act as if, I get a good lift.

I refuse to limit the outer boundaries of my potential until I collect some data.

Beliefs are limits . . . examine and go beyond.

When I believe, I usually receive.

I say I can to my dreams, even if they seem impossible.

The past is no valid indicator of what I can do in the present. I believe!

_____

_____

_____

_____

chapter II

Running in the Eye of a Hurricane

It is difficult to comprehend the quest of the mountain climber. Why would anyone want to put himself through such an ordeal? Climber-adventure runner Chris Reevley, who held the world record for the quickest ascent of the 22,834-foot peak Aconcagua in the Andes, spoke about why he loved to climb. He mentioned the stillness within; the single, focused mind; the moment when Zen meets the zone. Listening to him is a reminder of what we love about running—the opportunity to enter into the quiet single-mindedness where the moment-by-moment responsibilities in all of life, for the time being, are reduced to placing one foot ahead of the other as we listen to the inner rhythms of each step, of each heartbeat. Such narrowed focus and concentration helps to create a calm, safe place much like the eye of a hurricane, a miracle calm amid the chaos of the everyday world. The central nervous system seems to enjoy working with smaller targets.

Such single-minded focus is the basis of all excellence. Runners who become totally absorbed in what they are doing on the run are necessarily oblivious to those things that are not related to what they are doing. While a runner will be aware of (and reacts to) being passed by someone during a race, she may be oblivious to the crowd or what is going on in the high jump pit each time she passes it on the track. Such runners are childlike in their absolute absorption as they tune into their form, poise, and fluid movement. They run and get lost in the present. This oneness with running yields a high, a sense of being in a time warp, a flowing state without any conscious need to control; it's an ecstatic, trancelike level of concentration. You can feel things move along in a natural rhythm, the way they're supposed to. Have you ever run past certain familiar landmarks but were totally unaware of them as you glided by them? You were focused with a single mind.

Focusing is the process of narrowing your concentration to eliminate specific unproductive or distractive occurrences. It is a method of fine-tuning your span of attention so that you stay in the moment. Yet it is not easy to do. Why is it so difficult to focus? After all, babies easily focus intently on an item of interest without distraction. Observe a one-year-old pondering a toy sailboat floating in a tub. Noise or sound of any kind, including a call from the parents, won't take away the purposeful attention given to that boat. Have you tried calling to a child who is involved with an activity? Forget it! The reason young children can focus so well is

that they do not feel as though they are being evaluated. As adults, we quickly become aware that our performances are judged. Such evaluation diverts our attention.

Competition is traditionally an arena of extrinsic evaluation: places, times, distances, and all measurements of how you are performing. People are watching, and this can interfere with our abilities to focus, making it exponentially more challenging to perform up to our abilities. We become self-conscious, and this divides our attention between the audience and the task. When the mind becomes disconnected from the task, for whatever reason, the task becomes more difficult.

A talented high school runner who was experiencing this disconnection needed some mental strategies to help her regain her successful form from the previous year. She had been the league champ, undefeated in every meet before her senior year. After a lengthy discussion, it became quite clear that parental pressure to win and secure a college scholarship was a major distraction, the primary concern. Social and financial restrictions were punishments handed down to her by her parents to "help" her improve. Paradoxically, they forced her into a rebellious mode; she unconsciously began to sabotage her own efforts. Her mind was filled with chatter, and concentration was lost. It was the parents who needed help in understanding the dynamics of the situation. Once they did understand, they eventually backed off, and her ability to focus was recaptured. She began to excel once again as her mind became connected to the task rather than to the external parental pressure.

From what you have just read, it becomes clear that concentration is the learned skill of being alert to the task while simultaneously excluding negative external environmental factors and internal distraction. In the early stages of a race, an astute runner is like a camera focusing back and forth from narrow to broad, from internal to external. Internal factors include fears, expectations, fatigue, and doubt; external factors might be weather conditions, course terrain, lighting, the ubiquitous crowd, and other competitors. The objective of concentration is to focus your lens on what is important while minimizing the distraction. We will offer you practical, concrete ways to "park your attention" later in this chapter.

The specific neurophysiology of concentration has yet to be fully understood. But as we discussed in chapter 2, the limbic system and cerebral cortex both contribute to this behavior. Learning occurs when the "calming" cerebral cortex overrides the "instinctual" limbic system. The ability to learn new things, stay focused, and concentrate is enhanced by maintaining a calm state. This is easy during a nap, but is more difficult in the middle of a race.

Your experience with racing will help you to run smarter as you learn to develop ways of enhancing and controlling your focus. Practice the following focusing–calming procedures several times a week during your training, under a wide variety of training conditions (intense workouts, relaxed runs, intervals, hills, surges), and see if during the run your heart rate drops (by three to five beats), your respiration slows down (by three to five breaths per minute), and your perceived exertion (self-perceived effort) becomes easier.

Strengthen Your Focusing Attraction

Whatever you wish to concentrate on, create a way to become more attracted to it. For example, to focus more clearly on your stride, concentrate on your cadence or rhythmical beat each time your feet strike the ground. As a baseball player concentrating on hitting the ball focuses on the ball's red stitching or the printing on the leather, runners concentrating on form can often watch their shadows on the road (when the sun cooperates). You can also focus on arm swing, body posture, and, perhaps, the feet of the runner directly in front of you. Also, you can imagine your lungs expanding or heart pumping when concentrating on breathing or blood flow.

Internal Distraction—Learn to Focus Externally

When irrational fears, doubt, or fatigue creep into your thoughts, begin to focus externally upon the closest runner's feet and look for his left shoulder. Or, if you're sitting around waiting for an event to take place, relax and gain control over your environment; focus on a simple object like a stone or a blade of grass. Absorb its details—color, shape, and texture. Imagine yourself so small that you could hide behind the object. The purpose of this exercise is to take your mind away from the internal distraction by forcing attention to the outside.

External Distraction—
Learn to Focus Internally

When weather conditions, crowd noise, rough terrain, and other external distractions hinder your concentration, go into a relaxed state and begin to focus on your stride, breathing, or form. Make your attraction stronger using the procedure above.

Change Your Interpretation
of the Distraction

Remember that it is your view or interpretation of the distraction that makes it what it is. Rain may be an external distraction for many, yet those who run well in such conditions do not see it as a problem. You may try to reinterpret rain as flowing drops coating you with energy. When confronted with hills, see them as an opportunity to leave others behind because your opponents seem to become anguished at the sight of them. For this procedure to work, you must practice the reinterpretation prior to the event by anticipating possible distractions and changing your view of them. It is best done through a relaxation–visualization sequence. In your deeply relaxed state, imagine a scenario that has been a source of distraction. Then see and feel yourself running under similar conditions, having changed only your interpretation of it. For example, you may become nervous about the unfamiliarity of the race course because you didn't have a chance to get to know it earlier. Where are the big uphills, the long downhills, streams, sand mounds, or other difficult challenges? Know that you can never be fully aware of every course. Create an attitude in which you take on each unfamiliar new challenge on the course as an opportunity to display your greatness. Flow with the terrain. Adjust your stride for the long downhills, and pump up the arms on the steep climbs. Affirm that *New courses are my power* as you surge down the road to a strong finish. Tell yourself that you are comfortable whenever you run an unfamiliar course and that such situations will not detract from your performance. Naturally, if you have the chance to review the course prior to racing, you should take advantage of the opportunity.

The Isolation Camera

This exercise works well just prior to a race when you wish to keep your head together when all others are losing theirs. It is a process of selectively narrowing your attention from the wide world of competition to one specific aspect of your own performance. In a deep state of relaxation, begin to visualize the following sequence.

1. Think of a large circle. Within this circle, see many sports being played simultaneously in different segments of this area. Focus on each one individually, and then scan the space until you hit on another. Make believe you are a camera.

2. When you get to the track-and-field and distance runners section, see in your mind all of the activity going on. Someone is pole vaulting, others are sprinting, and still others are on the road running a 10K event; focus your camera within that circle.

3. After a few minutes of looking at that, focus on your event. Draw a circle around those participating, and as you watch, begin to see yourself emerge.

4. Draw a circle around only you and continue to see yourself as if a TV camera were isolating its focus on you. Watch yourself performing at your best.

5. Begin to focus on a part of your body (such as your heart) and narrow your concentration to that area. Draw a circle around that part of you, and notice everything down to the slightest detail. See the valves opening and the blood being pumped by the large, strong muscle. Stay with this picture for a few minutes.

6. Focus the camera on your feet and, in particular, your running shoes. Notice every slight detail of those shoes as you use the slow motion capability of your camera. See the impact of the shoe as the sole compresses against the road surface. Concentrate totally on your smooth, efficient stride and rhythmical cadence.

By "parking your attention" in this way, you will be able to block out all extrinsic distractions, relax, conserve energy for the race, and focus on the task of competition.

Explore the Distraction

You're running the first mile of a distance event and become distracted because you don't feel well; your breathing is off, and there is a general feeling of malaise. *Oh no!* you groan, and begin to lose concentration. When in the middle of such negative experiences, allow yourself to acknowledge and explore those feelings; try to focus on what they are asking you to do. Perhaps you need to manipulate your pace, stride, and form for a few minutes to see the reaction. Acknowledging these distractions will enable you to experience the normal cycles of competition; once you accept the situation, the distraction will ease up and your ability to focus will improve. This process of acceptance allows you to cope with the distraction without pushing it away.

Mantra Chanting

Many people in Eastern cultures have developed their skills of concentration by rhythmic breathing to chanted mantras. A mantra is a word or phrase repeated vocally or subvocally. The syllable *om* is an example of one you may recognize. Runners involved with transcendental meditation (TM) have found their mantras to be quite helpful to their ability to focus on the run. You can experiment with any phrase; try making it rhythmic to coincide with your stride. For example, the phrase *Run strong, run long* can be repeated one word per step.

As you can see, exercises in focusing and concentration are quite diverse. They seem rather simple, yet the results when practiced in training and racing regularly can be powerful. From what you have read, you can now see that there are ways that you can take control of those annoying and distracting situations, whether they are internal or external. The key to success is to remember that concentration is a constant vigil; do not leave it to chance.

Also, remember that learning to focus your mind requires practice and time. The mind will always wander, regardless of how much you practice and how mentally strong you are. It is impossible to remain permanently focused, particularly in the longer races. You may even look for opportunities to give your mind a break from the rigors of concentrating rather than trying to maintain your focus. For example, take a few minutes at mile 10 of a marathon and notice your competition, the surroundings, and the terrain. Notice the plane overhead and the birds landing on the phone wires. Think about your wonderful family or friends. Then, purposely having distracted yourself for a minute, return once again to the task at hand.

Visualization

In a deeply relaxed state with eyes closed, visualize the following to help gain greater control over distraction and focus on the task.

Imagine yourself running in an upcoming race.

Sense various distractions in your mind: noise, wind, rain, cramping.

Tell these distractions to leave, and immediately focus on stride, form, and breathing.

Feel yourself relax, and continue to concentrate on the rhythm of your run.

Stay with this image for two minutes if you can. If distracted, acknowledge it and just come back when you're ready.

Affirmations

Use these words as you visualize, create some of your own in the blanks, and be sure to recite them each day, particularly prior to an event.

Think less, achieve more.

Single-mindedness creates happiness.

Like a child at play, I ask my mind to stay.

Focus, focus, focus, and focus.

_____

_____

_____

_____

IV

Hurdling Obstacles
From Within

In part IV on the road to running within, you will be given the necessary strategies, tools, and shifts in attitude that will help you cope with the onset of inevitable problems and concerns that crop up during training and racing. Chapters 12, 13, and 14 will help you to examine and alter your psychological views of fatigue, overtraining, and injury, and mitigate their power over you. You will learn to embrace them as familiar friends who run with you and with anyone who chooses to push the envelope of performance. In chapter 15, we will bring you encouraging and inspirational information with regard to aging and performance by exploring and debunking many myths about aging that we have bought into and accepted as unquestionable truth. The psychophysiological evidence with regard to these taboo subjects is most compelling and helpful in mitigating the power that these so-called demons or obstacles seem to have over our performances. Instead, they become wonderful opportunities to facilitate our growth and development as athletes.

Flowing With Fatigue

W e call it the *fatigue intrigue*. Working with some of the best distance runners in this country, we notice that they are particularly captivated by the psychology of fatigue. As a runner who, like the elite, specializes in pushing your limits during a race, you often experience a visit from this painful friend, yet know very little about it other than it hurts and no one is spared.

Fatigue is always a factor in running. All athletes, regardless of their level of fitness, experience it when the envelope of limitlessness is being pushed. It is simply your body's positive way of talking to you, giving you information about training, nutritional needs, and mental conditioning. It is a necessary and essential element in the exploration of your full potential. Physiologists and athletes have asked the questions, *How fatigued do I need to be in order to improve my performances? How long will the process take, and how do I design and implement the workouts to achieve the desired results?* This chapter will help you learn to push yourself through your fatigue.

What Causes Fatigue?

Fatigue can be defined in many ways. For the purpose of this chapter, we focus on the short-term aspects of fatigue—that is, the fatigue that accumulates during strenuous efforts. In the next chapter, we examine the chronic effects of fatigue—also known as overtraining.

As we know it, fatigue has both a psychological and physiological component. When you deplete your glycogen stores, for example, you become physiologically tired. Your muscles become less fluid; they tighten up. The message goes to the brain, which in turn sabotages the body's efforts by sending negative messages to stop or back off: *Let him go, fifth place isn't that bad; Wouldn't it be great to be swimming? Why am I doing this?* Such thoughts are familiar to most of us during moments of extreme exertion. What is holding you back? Your mind or your body? Why do you feel fatigued? Is it mental exhaustion or lactic acid accumulation in the blood and muscles? How do we determine when it is okay for our minds to tell our bodies to push the limit? Pay close attention to your perceived effort, and try to find the delicate balance between the speed that extends you yet is comfortable. Make small adjustments in stride length, arm swing, and breathing. See if you can adjust your speed, absorb the fatigue, and continue the rest of the run at a competitive pace, while carrying the fatigue.

From an exercise physiologist's perspective, if your heart rate and breathing are not excessively high and your running form is preserved while your mind is focused, then push your effort to the point where you nearly lose control of your form and your effort feels extremely hard. Sometimes you may even become upset and anxious about the fact that you are becoming physically fatigued. Such secondary anxiety can lead you to get angry. You begin to think, *I was feeling so good; why is this happening to me?* Attention to any of these inner sensations will distract you, create more anxiety, impede your performance, frustrate your efforts to continue, and create greater fatigue.

Fatigue can also be triggered by the mind before the body is actually ready to become tired. How many times have you been running along smoothly in a race, when suddenly an unanticipated hill appears and fatigue mysteriously sets in? Or maybe an unexpected headwind greets you at the turnaround point. Perhaps you have found yourself getting tired after being passed by a runner you knew you could beat. These situations create another anxiety syndrome, which can lead to negative physiological reactions that cause further fatigue. Neurophysiologically, this is a result of an internal panic in the limbic system. The negative emotions cause facial frowning, hunching of the shoulders, and reduction in arm swing, all of which eventually reduce breathing capacity. Limbic system override can precipitate tenseness, a misstep, a fall, a choke, and in rare circumstances, a full-blown panic attack.

Strategies to Cope With Fatigue

During a race, you can't take time to rest, but you may be able to cope more productively with the tension, anxiety, and stress created by the onset of fatigue. You can do this by yielding to your fatigue in the spirit of *wu wei*, which in Chinese means, among other things, *don't force.* Fighting or becoming angry at fatigue causes tension, frustrates or distracts you, and makes you lose your confidence, enthusiasm, and courage—all of which further your fatigue.

Consider this story as an example of wu wei in action. A 45-minute 10K runner was 30 minutes into a grueling race when her body began to cramp. The tightness and loss of fluidity made her feel quite anxious. Thoughts of dropping out and not finishing the race began to play tricks with her prerace confidence. Then she remembered a strategy she had learned from a friend to let go and talk to this distraction: *Hi, fatigue . . . it's you again. I'm busy right now . . . got a job to complete. If you want to hang around, you can, but I won't have time for you until I finish.* As silly as this may appear, her acknowledgment of the fatigue enabled her to laugh, relax, concentrate on the race, and feel more in control. She chose the path of least resistance by yielding to the rigid onslaught of fatigue and remembered that with fatigue, as with any force, resistance is futile.

Another practical tip for runners comes from exercise physiology experiments measuring blood lactic acid accumulations during progressive exercise. Because blood lactate (lactic acid in the blood) can suddenly rise to high levels, athletes should carefully monitor their race pace and perceived exertion. When you feel too fatigued, first slow down slightly and focus on relaxing the body in order to bring the necessary slowdown. Then focus on slowing your breathing while maintaining a competitive stride. Many times you will discover that very slight changes in pace can yield large improvements in perceived effort. This occurs because the blood lactate can increase and decrease at an exponential rate with these changes in pace. In the case of a runner, as the exercise gets more demanding, the rate of lactic acid production increases until the muscles can no longer keep up with energy metabolism.

There are other strategies that have been helpful in our work with elite runners. The following methods are among the best available; use these tips to help you work with your fatigue rather than push it away (as if you could). Remember that by training yourself to deal with fatigue, you likely will have an edge over your competition.

• When fatigue sets in, rather than obsess about how far you have to go, focus on small, manageable segments. Tell yourself, for example, *I'll just do this next loop;* or the next mile, the next stretch, and so on. Mentally break up your task into pieces, and visualize each piece as part of a beautiful mosaic that you are creating. If you know there are 3 miles to go, run 1 mile and do it

three times, re-evaluating your condition at each checkpoint. Doing this will help to relax you and infuse hope back into your nervous system.

• Concentrate on your form and pace. This is a method Jon Sinclair, one of the best and most consistent elite runners of all time, endorses. Ask yourself, *Am I going too fast at this point? How is my stride? Should I adjust my knee lift?* Elite runners prefer to associate with what's going on in the body as opposed to disassociating from it by thinking of dinner plans, work, the pain of running, or any other item in their lives that redirects their attention elsewhere. By paying attention to their bodies, they are able to correct errors and reduce fatigue that may be due to an inefficient running style. Concentrate on your mechanics instead of becoming anxious over discomfort. Such a task-centered approach allows you to remain focused on the race and prevents you from being distracted by the pain.

• Research shows that our bodies respond physiologically to the images our minds hold for a particular situation. For example, an image of a lemon triggers salivation. Imagining an exciting moment in your life may trigger a galvanic skin response (goose bumps). Because mental images can stimulate the body to produce beneficial changes, using visualization techniques can help you work with your fatigue. For example, during the weeks preceding the event, simulate the race in your mind and imagine the scenario of fatigue coming on at a point in the race. What do you do to work with this fatigue positively? Visualize running smoothly, effortlessly, and full of energy. Try imagining the tightness in the shoulder muscles dissipating as you relax and drop your arms for 30 seconds. Visualize the tight muscles as small blocks of snow quickly melting away. Focus on relaxing your face muscles, and notice how fatigue begins to fade away. By rehearsing dealing with this fatigue, we will be ready to put this plan into action during the race.

• Change your old habitual beliefs about fatigue and pain. For clarity, we define these beliefs collectively as muscle soreness or feelings of excessive strain on the heart and lungs. Under this definition, fatigue and pain fall under what we consider physiological limits. This is clearly different than the focal pain associated with an injury. Research shows that if you change your beliefs about physiological limits, you will change the pain's effect on you. For example, interpret it simply as a feeling you get when your muscles are working hard. See it as an important indication that you are exploring the outer boundaries of your running potential. Think about how necessary fatigue is if you wish to experience significant breakthroughs in your performance. Fatigue is there because you are exploring your potential and giving your best effort. It is like a good training partner, there to help you grow and expand as a competitive athlete. When you create this shift in consciousness, notice how there is a subsequent shift in the fatigue as well.

• Get a reality check! When fatigued, there is the tendency to feel self-pity and think you're alone. Look around and acknowledge what the elite runner does: everyone hurts; we all are feeling pain. When in a race, remember that to compete means *to seek together.* We all seek our greatness and together experience fatigue as our companion on the trail of optimal performance. This in itself is what bonds us all together.

• Divert your mind. A 50-year-old 2:50 marathoner we know chants, sings, and thinks about his work when he trains and races. Others claim to fantasize about a trip, plan for the future, or solve problems. A top female runner discloses that she squeezes her thumbs against her index fingers until her attention is completely focused on the pain in her fingers; she then shakes her hands to release the pressure, and fatigue seems to leave her body. Try chanting a mantra like *I go with the flow like H_2O,* or *I feel great, I feel smooth* to self-direct your thoughts to the positive. Remember from chapter 4 that words directly influence our reality; keep them positive.

You have many alternatives for coping with fatigue. Give each one a try in various training and racing situations to see what works best for you. Record the methods you try in your logbook, and note which works best. Prior to each race or run, mentally prepare the strategies you will employ. Knowing that you are in control will stall the anxiety and lessen fatigue. At the first hint of heavy legs, put your strategies to work. Keep in mind that you can take charge of fatigue; you need not suffer through it. Remember to pay close attention to your breathing rate, foot strike mechanics, running pace, and perceived exertion. Performing small, frequent adjustments in running speed may prevent you from overfatiguing.

Visualization

Because your body directly responds physiologically to the images your mind holds, choose those that help you feel relaxed and fluid and lessen the fatigue brought on by prerace anxiety and tension. Do the following visualization exercise for two minutes a day for a minimum of seven days prior to competition to help you gain greater control over the fatigue you invariably will experience.

Imagine that fatigue sets in with a few miles to go in the race.

Feel the legs getting heavy, the arms falling to the sides.

Notice the anxiety of not being able to finish set in.

Talk to your fatigue, befriend it.

Feel your whole body beginning to relax.

Feel energized as you start to run smoothly, fluidly.

Imagine seeing the finish line, and feel elation.

Cross the line tired, yet exhilarated.

Affirmations

Use these phrases during your visualization, create some of your own, and recite all of them each day.

Fatigue is my friend, I embrace it for all it's worth.

When fatigue sets in, I yield and go with the flow.

Fatigue is an opportunity to tune in to my body and make corrections.

Change the image, change the pain.

I'm tired, yet I know I'm not alone.

_____

_____

_____

_____

chapter 13

Gaining Without Straining

One of our most difficult tasks in working with running clients is to temper their zealous enthusiasm for their sport. So many, driven to excel, become slaves to the adage *No pain, no gain* as they train harder, not smarter. On the brink of exhaustion, they walk the fine line between not enough and disaster as they risk becoming imbalanced both psychologically and physiologically. The medical problems usually begin with musculoskeletal over-use injury and progress to gastrointestinal disturbances, poor sleep, decreased appetite, weight changes, and mood alterations. In more severe cases, the neurotransmitters of the hypothalamus and the pituitary hormones become asynchronous. This can produce depression, chronic fatigue, loss of libido, postural hypotension (dizziness when standing), and, in women, amenorrhea (temporary loss of a menstrual cycle). Symptoms may carry on for months to years if not treated with appropriate rest recovery. Excessiveness with running regimens can cause extreme chronic fatigue (unlike the fatigue that accumulates during strenuous efforts), illness, injury, and mental and physical burnout. Excess can strip you of the vibrance, vitality, and wellness accrued from this healthy, invigorating sport.

Runners are likely candidates for indulging in extremes if they adhere to the faulty notion that more is better. A national-class marathoner was getting excellent results from his 110-miles-per-week training program. He began to win numerous races and attract much attention. He reasoned that if he got to this level by doing this much work, he'd be much better if he increased his mileage by 40 to 50 miles each week. He followed this logic, self-destructed, never recovered, and eventually quit running altogether. The problem for all of us is that the mind is always ready to tell the body to do more than it can handle. However, by recording and interpreting physiologic data such as your morning resting heart rate, perceived exertion during submaximal runs, and time trial performances, you can learn to design proper training programs for yourself. (This is where a knowledgeable coach can help.)

However, once you reach a certain amount of training, the gain that your body may experience from doing higher-volume or higher-intensity workouts is drastically offset by the accumulation of tightness, tension, stress, imbalance, and fatigue that wear your body down. By overtraining, you create a debt due to the constant withdrawals from your energy levels. This debt needs to be paid back with rest, or you will eventually become physically and emotionally bankrupt.

A good rule of thumb to help avoid overtraining is to balance any increase in training with a comparable increase in recovery and rest. For example, exercise physiology researchers have found that one day of hard training should be followed by two easy days. Similarly, three to six weeks of progressive buildup should be followed by one to two weeks of easy training or tapering. Athletes vary greatly in their ability to adapt to exercise. When travels, illnesses, or other unplanned circumstances add to your daily stress, it is critical that you reduce training and take adequate rest.

Signals of Overtraining

The signs of being excessive with your running training are often subtle and insidious in nature, catching up with you before you realize it. By then it is too late—the amount you have overdrawn has taken its toll. The key to successful management of your training is to identify the early warning signs of overdoing it. If any of the following physiological or psychological symptoms persist over a prolonged period, you may be in danger of overtraining, which will result in burnout, injury, or illness. (The psychological symptoms are more subtle.)

Physiological signals

- Poor quality or restless sleep night after night
- Frequent minor bodily accidents, such as cuts, bumps, sprains, strains, and bruises
- Constant and frequent colds or flu
- Drastic changes in appetite
- Constipation or diarrhea
- Frequent mood shifts
- Nightmares
- Dizziness with standing (postural hypotension)
- Low back pain
- Constant fatigue

- Heavy sensation in legs
- Muscle and joint pains
- Lymph gland swelling
- Loss of menstruation (women)
- Impaired physical performance
- Weight loss

Psychological signals

- Difficulty making decisions that would normally be easy
- Excessive daydreaming
- Sudden increase in drug consumption (coffee included—sorry!)
- Excessive worrying, especially over trivial events
- Mistrust of friends
- Missing appointments and deadlines
- Forgetting or confusing dates and times
- Feelings of worthlessness
- Brooding over failing to attain goals
- Sudden reversal of usual patterns of behavior
- Loss of libido

Changing Course

Overtraining, in a spiritual sense, is a cancer of the running soul. It knocks you off balance, forces you to lose perspective with your running, and destroys your appreciation of its essence—the beauty, the flow, the enjoyable movement of your body over the terrain. The perfect treatment for the illness is to fortify yourself with *moderation* and inoculate your consciousness with a dose of *less is more.* Temporarily reducing your training load will alleviate the fatigue and make you suddenly begin to appear fitter and faster.

When this disease of excessiveness goes into remission, you will begin to feel the physical, mental, emotional, and spiritual benefits. Excitement, joy, enthusiasm, and satisfaction will return. Moderation, the flowing dance between two extremes, is food for the running soul; it is a gain-without-strain approach that makes you feel alive and perfectly aligned with your happier self.

By so doing, you enhance your overall training and attain not only the psychological advantages of moderation, but also the numerous physiological benefits by giving your body the chance to recuperate and become even stronger.

At some point during your running career, there's a good chance that your interest in the sport will wane, boredom will set in, and your motivation to get out the door and get that run in will be nonexistent. This periodic loss of interest is natural and can be attributed to many factors, most of which point to the absence of pleasure and joy in the day-to-day task—the most important motivating factors in running.

High mileage, week after week, catches up with the best of us. If injury doesn't affect your motivation, then mental fatigue certainly will. Pounding the roads each day can be, quite frankly, boring. Many neophytes to the sport can't get enough of their addiction to running and burn out emotionally. One beginning runner, after only six months of running, began to take to the roads twice a day to get his mileage up. He did his second workout at night in front of a friend's car on the side of the road as the lights shone the way. After a few months of this routine, he quit suddenly and did not run a step for the next eight months. After his long hiatus, he returned to the track, where he ran only three times a week and remained very excited. He was fortunate enough to have learned from his radical running behavior that moderation and consistency were the key for him—he didn't get burned out, but maintained and improved his fitness. Look for ways to create a planned pause in your training regime: one day off a week, one week off a month, one month off a year will enable you to renew your motivation. The possibilities of creating pauses are unlimited, as will be your level of motivation.

Often the anhedonic nature of training regimens can be blamed for waning motivation with running. Quite simply, ask yourself, *Where is the fun of the run?* If none exists, look for ways to build fun *into* the run. That's right; the run should be fun while you're doing it, not just when it is over. Seriousness is epidemic in the running community. The attitude from many runners with long faces is, *This is serious business. I'm training, it necessarily hurts, and there's no time to smile.* Little do they know that frowning creates tension throughout the entire body, making one tired. Once again, Fred Rohé, in *The Zen of Running,* captures the essence of this feeling:

. . . if the dance of the run isn't fun
then discover another dance, because
without fun the good of the run
is undone, and a suffering runner
always quits, sooner or later.

One of the best ways to experience more joy and fun on the run is to realize that any changes in routine or environment result in increased interest and motivation, and, subsequently, improved performance. If you are discouraged in your running, evaluate your training. Are you running with a fixed, minimal repertoire of workouts in a repetitive fashion? Facing such boredom would test the most compulsive, committed runner. Any slight change in your workout regimen can sufficiently excite you to run again.

Vary Your Workouts

Rather than running your miles at the same pace each day, change your speed: run slow for a while, then switch to a faster pace. Or run two short workouts today, one long one tomorrow; run alone today, tomorrow try it with a friend or group; try some intervals for a workout; alternate walking and running, and see how far you can go before tiring; try running during different times of the day; make the workout meaningful by aligning it with one of your goals (running a faster 5 miles, for example). There are endless variations if you use your imagination.

The possibilities become even more interesting if you vary the environment where you run as well as the workout itself. Until you are capable of running higher mileage, you may have to drive to another location—but the rewards are worth it. Running on a track every day is emotionally tiring and probably boring as well. Try going up some hills. You might run slower, but the benefits will be greater and your enthusiasm will soar—strengthening your body, mind, and spirit. If it's hills today, do some roadwork tomorrow. If there are some well-defined trails around, you and a friend may want to explore them together. If you're visiting a friend in another town, bring running gear and discover the area by going for a run after you arrive. When you have a particularly good run, remember where it was and return in a few days. You'll be amazed how exciting it will feel to go back for more fun. If you plan properly the night before, you will find your motivation level

Photo © Ron Dahlquist

quite high as you look forward to a "new" workout. Finally, don't overlook the possibility of a few days off in your schedule as a technique to increase your hunger for running.

Regardless of your choice, the more playful and childlike your runs become, the better your mental outlook will be toward continuing your efforts. For example, try leaving your watch at home and forget about recording miles. Run home from the movies instead of walking or taking a bus. Take the bus outbound from your house, and then run home.

Embrace the Health Benefits

The bottom line of why most of us begin and continue to run seems to be physiological in nature. Keep your dreams of a healthier, happier life alive and vivid by simply posting a list on the refrigerator door of the physiological benefits that can be gained from running. This visual reminder will help keep in perspective those important intrinsic reasons for loving your efforts. Some of the specific intrinsic health benefits you may wish to list include the following.

Improved blood pressure control. With regular running, you experience increased blood vessel size, number, and elasticity, all factors involved in controlling blood pressure.

Better blood quality. Through regular running, you increase the number of red blood cells, hemoglobin, and plasma (the liquid portion of blood) in your blood. An increase in the red cell mass improves the oxygen-carrying capacity of the blood. Plasma volume increases expand the volume of the exercising muscles (pumped-up muscles). Also, the blood's ability to dissolve clots (called the blood's *fibrinolytic response*) will improve.

Prevention of diabetes mellitus. Regular exercise is fundamental in improving blood sugar control. Additionally, a therapeutic exercise program can prevent Type II diabetes, which is associated with obesity and aging.

Prevention of cancer. The most current studies indicate that a lifelong regular exercise program can reduce your chances of colon, breast, and reproductive organ cancers.

Healthier pregnancies for women. Higher levels of fitness seem to improve pregnancy and delivery outcomes. It is now well established that women can safely exercise during pregnancy. Interestingly, several female athletes have set world records after becoming mothers.

Improved blood lipid profile. All forms of regular exercise can improve your blood lipid profile. Research shows that aerobic exercise can *raise* your HDLC (high-density lipoprotein cholesterol), called the *good cholesterol* since it collects fat in the body and delivers it to the liver for conversion into energy. Exercise can also *lower* your triglycerides, a component of the bad fats in the blood.

Improved immune system. Regular moderate exercise will improve your body's ability to fight off cancer and infections. It is important to note, however, that periodic strenuous exercise temporarily suppresses your immune system for several days.

Stronger heart. Like any muscle, the heart will grow larger and stronger if it's worked. Running regularly will help the heart to become more efficient and effective.

More efficient lungs. When you stress the lungs through aerobic exercise, they open up and flush out, using more air space. Running helps to reduce the effects of asthma and emphysema.

Improved muscle tone. With regular exercise, your body begins to look aesthetically more appealing as muscles develop better tone and definition.

Stronger bones. Osteoporosis is a bone-weakening condition resulting from a severe decrease in bone density, and it often results in bone fractures. Healthy running and exercise control bone mineral loss, essential in the treatment of osteoporosis.

Improved sleep. Regular exercise improves the quality of sleep in most individuals. Additionally, most runners report ease with falling asleep simply because they feel tired from the day's exercise.

Weight control. Exercise speeds up metabolism, suppresses the appetite, and burns fat, helping you maintain a healthy body weight.

Reduced effects of aging. Regular exercise increases the strength and endurance of the skeletal muscles and the heart at any age. Studies reveal that lifelong exercise increases your life expectancy and improves your functional capacity as a senior citizen. Regular exercise also helps prevent the risk of chronic illnesses associated with aging.

Become Affiliated

Since recognition by others is a strong extrinsic motivator, we suggest becoming affiliated with a local running group or club. By so doing, you'll meet other runners of your caliber, receive pertinent information about seminars and clinics, and expand your social contacts. Knowing, for instance, that you're racing for a team can motivate you to maintain a higher level of fitness. Of course, be aware that there is a danger of feeling too much pressure to perform; this can contribute to burnout and loss of motivation. Use the group to motivate you to do track workouts or run on a rainy day. Just knowing that they are there can encourage you to get out of bed and show up. Most clubs have newsletters; this is one way of getting your name in print, either through your race results or by your writing a column. Some clubs also have annual award ceremonies to recognize various runners' accomplishments throughout the year.

Give Yourself a Reality Check

Often, it's difficult to motivate yourself to run because you feel tired after a full day's work. The fatigue you experience may very well be mental—you've been using the brain for hours. But once you get going, your body comes alive. If the thought of running 5 or more miles seems overwhelming during these moments, make an agreement with yourself; just run for 4 minutes, and if things aren't looking better at the end of that time, turn around and run home. By the time you reach the door, you will have completed a mile, more or less; if the "fatigue" has been shaken, keep going. If not, you can write it off, stay inside, and use this time to stretch, read, and relax; tomorrow's another day. Your body will thank you for the break.

Set the Stage for Success

Many runners place unrealistic demands and set heroic expectations on their performances. This sets the stage for failure as they find themselves dreading the chore of following through on such promises. This drop in passion and motivation is accompanied by frustration, and the desire to pursue any running goals is eventually lost. Remember that if you keep the training program pleasurable and rewarding for yourself, your interest will continue to flourish. The success created as a result of reaching realistic expectations will enhance your motivation.

Substitute Alternative Training Methods

Runners are beginning to discover that cycling and swimming can enhance their fitness, give the legs a much-deserved rest, and provide a psychological break from the running routine. This periodic rest from running also contributes to the maintenance of a healthy level of motivation. World-class runners like Frank Shorter have used the bike as an adjunct to their fitness program. Taking time away from running can increase your passion to get back into it. By the way, an intense workout on a bike for 25 miles is the approximate equivalent of a strenuous 10-mile run, without the pounding. (The conversion factor of cycling distance to running distance is 2.5 to 1.)

© Terry Wild

Stop Running

When all else fails, back off completely from running until you have the desire again. This usually becomes necessary when you overlook our suggestion earlier in this chapter to build in pauses. What do you have to lose? Right now, you are becoming supersaturated and need a break.

When should you start in again after a layoff? The time to begin running is when you get "that feeling." Thoughts like *What a great day for a run* will give you a clue. The first three days may be the most difficult, as you may experience withdrawal or guilt. It gets easier each day after that as you discover how wonderful it is to have so much extra free time. My (Jerry's) last cold turkey experience lasted 18 days. I biked and swam only if I cared to, and refused to read running books and magazines. On the 19th day, I remember getting an urge to run on the beach. I followed that craving and enjoyed every step of the run. Three days later I entered a crazy mountain race (no time pressure, as the distance was an oddball 5.83 miles and the terrain was vicious) and ran a faster time than I had two years previously on the same course. I do think that the cycling I did in my no-run phase helped, as well as having a relaxed mental framework.

You may find that many of the motivational strategies listed above overlap and reinforce each other. For example, the combination of becoming affiliated with a running group or training partner, creating changes in your training program, and keeping in mind the physiological benefits of the sport may help ignite your passion and a higher level of motivation. The key is to try initiating those factors that are absent when interest is low. Remember that if you want to increase your level of motivation, if you become too intense or too serious, other problems will arise comparable to severe burnout. If you find that you take yourself too seriously, lighten up and have a good time. Keeping perspective on how you feel, your attitudes and values, and your state of mind will prove to be important in your motivation and love for running. The neurophysiology of motivation has everything to do with the pleasure principle. Pleasurable behaviors are rewarded (subconsciously and consciously), and we tend to seek out situations that help us to engage in pleasure-producing behavior.

Remember that much of your interest will dwindle if you become too obsessed with what you love. There's nothing like a good vacation, away from mundane realities, to rekindle the love of what you do. A weekend trip to a place near your home without running can open your mind and clear your head. Try a sports weekend, or a tennis, volleyball, or basketball camp or clinic. Take a yoga or dance class, something to get you out of your set running routine, even if the new activity seems slightly odd for you.

The idea is to rest now or be forced to rest extensively at a later date. *Stress, then rest* is a good guide for moderation. We know that truly good music is the result of the *space* between the notes. Musical pauses are not a lack of action, they are an integral part of the action. So it is with your running regime. Getting in good shape is the result of the *rest* (pause) or space between the workouts—this rest allows your muscles and tissues to regenerate after the necessary "breakdown" of these tissues during training. Your cellular structure is fragile and requires periods of rest.

Olympian and author Jeff Galloway seems to understand the concept of moderation, having created a successful nationwide program for low-mileage marathon training. His running groups span 40 cities and have a membership of over 5,000. Where typically only one out of four people who begin training for the marathon ever finish one, Jeff's legions—using a modified low-mileage, minimalist, three-times-a-week, group-oriented, running-with-walking approach—experience a 98 percent success rate.

These participants say that one of the benefits of this program of moderation is that it gives them time to do other things in their lives while training seriously for a demanding event. They appreciate a balanced existence because it keeps them motivated on a daily basis. You may want to reevaluate your running program and adopt a more moderate approach such as Galloway's. If you decide to do so, consider the following mind-sets as strategies to help you along the way.

Cooperate With Your Natural Rhythms

There are natural cycles throughout each 12-month period that your body follows—like it or not. I (Jerry) fought this again and again until injury and illness forced a halt to my passion. When I tried to train continually at high levels, my body simply quit. I began to make changes by honoring the natural cycles, and made my workouts more low-key more often. As a result, my performance began to improve radically. Notice your peaks, valleys, and plateaus, and train accordingly; cut back, run with less intensity or less speed, or cross-train. Choreograph a yearly plan, and cooperate with the changes of your seasons and rhythms. Give yourself permission to swim downstream, to take the trail of least resistance; in doing so, you run with less risk of injury. Building a program based on six-month training cycles spread out over several years and punctuated with the key competitive events may be a way to go.

Effort Without Effort

The anxiety and tension a runner feels about having to exert a huge effort is a set-up for injury; such stress about performance tightens the muscles, with a subsequent decrease in the synchronicity between the hamstrings and the quadriceps—and then injury is not far behind. This brings us back again to the rule: rather than running harder, focus on running smarter—use your mind to focus on your body's movements. For example, when running a steep hill, rather than push or force your way up, relax your face and glide to the top. Think about your shoulders being lifted by helium balloons.

All-out efforts create pressure that is contrary to what you wish to accomplish. Remember from chapter 2 Coach Bud Winter's use of the 90 percent law. He found that athletes who ran with 90 percent effort were more relaxed, ran faster, and rarely got injured. Notice how championship performance in any sport always seems effortless. Athletes who have run world records or personal bests report that it "felt easy" not only because their bodies were highly tuned, but because they felt more relaxed and in control. This easy effort is the result of proper balancing of mind and body. At optimal levels of performance, all bodily systems are maximally efficient. This allows greater power output (running faster) for a given unit of muscle energy. Perfect blending of mind and body clearly produces a more efficient physiological running state.

Elite marathoners and national distance champions admit that the way to prevent overtraining is to focus on being relaxed rather than on exerting more power or effort. Relaxed running reduces fatigue, lowers stress, and improves coordination of the muscles, resulting in less chance of overuse injury.

Keep It Simple

In today's high-tech world of running, we reap the benefits of mechanical devices, yet forget to listen to our bodies. For example, we often become compulsive, trying to beat the watch when the body is screaming to stop. The device dictates the run, and the body becomes the slave to technology. Take a close look at your training program and search for ways to simplify. What's essential? What's not? Would it be helpful to have less to worry about? The complexity of gear and sophisticated training regimes could be distracting, forcing you to overtrain. We tend to be more relaxed and fluid when life is simple. Maybe we need to learn to run simply so that we can simply run.

For 55 years, Derek Turnbull has carried out this philosophy. He is a dedicated runner and sheep farmer from New Zealand who follows a very simple training program. Run around the farm, uphill, downhill, slow, and fast. He trains without a coach or much sophistication. Derek may be one of the greatest runners of the century. In 1992, at age 66, he set seven world records—in the 800-meter, 1500-meter, mile, 3000-meter, 5000-meter, 10,000-meter, and a 2:41:57 world record at the London Marathon to finish the season. Based on age-adjusted calculations, all of his world records exceed the 100 percent age-level value. This means his times are better than the theoretical (calculated) optimal performance norms for his age group.

Listening to Your Body With Resting Heart Rate

There is no need to be hooked up to biofeedback equipment or call the doctor to determine how your body is dong. To self-diagnose whether you are overtraining, when to run and when not to run, use the following simple, effective strategy as part of your daily routine along with your physical and mental training program.

1. For two weeks, before jumping out of bed, record your resting heart rate in your training log. Place two fingers on the pulse in your wrist or neck. Count the number of beats for 30 seconds, multiply that number by two, and record the product each day. Take the average over the 14-day span. Note that medications can alter the accuracy of your measurements. Additionally, proper fluid balance is essential for meaningful results. Drink enough liquids to produce copious clear urine.

2. Now that you have a baseline average, continue to take a reading each day in the same way. If your resting heart rate increases by 10 or more beats per minute on a given day, you should rest. If the rate is off by even 4 or 5 beats, you may want to do an easy workout that day. The idea is to not resume your usual workouts until the pulse settles down to its normal range. This means you have recovered.

Visualization

In your relaxed state, with your eyes closed, use this exercise to help you guard against excessiveness.

Imagine beginning one of your favorite runs.

Start out slowly, then pick up the pace.

Feel healthy and strong as you glide over the terrain.

Finish the run, and feel the fatigue from a good workout.

Notice how good it feels to rest and back off the next day.

Imagine your body fully recovered, and welcome the chance to run well again.

See yourself as a vibrant athlete, excited and enthused for your runs.

Feel mentally and physically fresh each day.

Affirmations

Use these as part of your visualization, create some of your own in the blanks, and recite them each day.

I realize my dreams when I avoid the extremes.

Moderation is the key to consistent optimal performance.

Excel without excess.

Stress, then rest.

Less is more.

_____

_____

_____

_____

Embracing Your Injury

The experienced runner respectfully appreciates the natural cycles of health and injury. One can do little to totally reverse this cycle, other than to wait it out and look for wisdom in acceptance of these times.

In this paraphrased statement from the ancient Chinese Book of Change, the *I Ching,* a more gentle mind-set will help you effectively cope with the shattering news of running injury if it occurs. Accepting injury when it happens is your body's way to take a break and then look to health with rest and time. It seems as though this 2,500-year-old wisdom has endured time and is, perhaps, more relevant for today's distance runner that ever before. According to this ancient wisdom, we need to nurture the mind and body and accept the situation at hand. In this chapter, we help you to become more aware of the ways to cope and accept this demon, and offer specific strategies that enable you to lower the incidence of running-related injury.

The incidence of running-related trauma is on the rise, and it is estimated that each year 5 to 6 million of us sustain a serious enough injury that warrants special care. It's a natural occurrence, but we do have some control over its intensity, seriousness, and frequency.

Controlling the Incidence of Injury

Sports medicine research reveals that most running injuries are related to overuse. Too many miles, too hard, too soon, and too frequently; as well as hill work, weight training, and cross-training, all contribute to a runner's training volume. Progressive buildup without proper adaptation overloads the tissues, and they eventually break down. Although this chapter emphasizes coping while injured, there are a few recommendations we can make to help lower the incidence of injury.

- Carefully plan your training program and adjust the workouts according to your body's response.
- Pay close attention to your morning resting heart rate, perceived exertion during exercise, appetite, sleep quality, and mood as discussed in the previous chapter on overtraining.

At the hint of the slightest twinge in your body, take a day or two off and cut back on intensity the next few runs.

- Changing the terrain can also give a nagging pain some relief. For example, if you have soreness in your Achilles tendon, stay away from hills and speed workouts.
- Focus on slowly and gently stretching your body daily. Bob Anderson's book *Stretching* is an excellent source for runners.

Dealing With Your Emotions When Injured

Injury and illness can turn an athlete's world upside-down—not only physically, but emotionally as well. When sudden injury or illness occurs, runners experience every emotion in the psychological lexicon: depression, anger, fear, tension, disgust, anxiety, and panic, to name a few. Such feelings, it has been shown, create psychophysiological reactions that contribute to and exacerbate the pain of the injury. When first injured, we usually go through a predictable sequence of five emotional reactions:

1. **Denial.** You say *No, not me . . . there's no problem . . . it'll go away.* When reality hits, the next stage makes its abrupt appearance.
2. **Anger.** *Why me . . .why now, damn it?* are words that usher in panic, which intensifies the pain; your anger often arises due to your inability to perform optimally, if at all.
3. **Bargaining.** *If I recover, I'll never do that again.* But this does little good to relieve the pain.
4. **Depression.** Realizing that the injury is really serious (you will not be able to run for awhile), you may withdraw and focus on self-pity.
5. **Acceptance.** *I'm injured, but I must go on with my life.* This is when the healing usually begins to take place.

Many runners alternate among these stages until they achieve acceptance of their injury. Once you accept that you are injured and need to take time off from running, you may have many questions that, if unanswered, can lead to much frustration and fear.

When will I run again?

Is the injury more serious than it appears?

How will I get by until then?

Where can I get help?

How long will this last?

Whether verbalized or not, the questions are there. Try to obtain satisfactory responses to these concerns and address the feelings of fear and panic with someone who is informed, experienced, and trained in these areas—another runner, a sports psychologist, or a sports physician can be helpful. Resolving your feelings will relieve much anxiety and facilitate a quick recovery process. Communicating in this way helps you release tension and demonstrates that you are not alone; it will also help you to maintain your identity as a runner and your connection with any running partners you have.

It may also be of help to know that some of the world's greatest athletes have recovered completely from injury. Distance star Joan Benoit Samuelson came back 17 days after knee surgery to win the Olympic trials in the marathon. World-class marathoner Toshihiko Seko, following a two-year bout with injury, returned to uncork a superb 2:08:35 race, 22 seconds off the world record at that time. American Olympian Paul McMullen cut off parts of two toes in a lawnmower accident. He resumed running three months after the accident, and nine months after the accident won the indoor nationals mile.

You may become inspired by these courageous efforts and return to peak form, setting PRs for all your distances. However, don't start back doing too much too fast; rest your injury and rehabilitate it by strengthening what needs to be strengthened, following doctor's orders, and keeping your focus on regaining your earlier form. If you can maintain some level of cardiovascular fitness while you're injured, you'll be able to recover and regain your overall fitness more quickly than if you don't. If your injury doesn't preclude you from pool running, stationary bike riding, or using a rowing machine, you can use these types of exercise to keep your body somewhat fit while recovering from your injury.

Physiologists and other sports medicine professionals have coined this the *Zatopek phenomenon* in honor of the great Czech

runner Emil Zatopek. In 1950, he was hospitalized for two weeks
prior to the European games due to food poisoning. He did not
train these two weeks. He was released two days prior to the
10,000-meter race, which he easily won by a full lap. Several days
later, he won the 5,000-meter race, improving his time by 23
seconds. His performance demonstrates how forced rest can
relieve high levels of fatigue, thereby unmasking one's true fitness
level. Of course, we must remember that because he was in such
good shape before the two weeks off training, he was able to come
back quickly. In his case, the rest acted as a forced taper.

The Body–Mind–Spirit Connection and Injury

Injury treatment is looked upon by many as a physical problem only. Sports medicine professionals use drugs, surgery, and structural manipulation—any of which may be indicated, but not to the exclusion of the crucial role of the mind in the process.

For treatment to be effective, the body and mind must work together as a team to facilitate complete recovery. Well-known author and former professor at UCLA Medical School Norman Cousins believed that physicians working with ill and injured patients must make careful estimates of the mind-set and emotional needs of the patient in order to be effective. Failure to do so will retard effective treatment, if not preclude it completely.

It is important to be aware of the impact of the psychological components of treating a physical injury. In addition to implementing the strategies provided in this book for dealing with injuries, finding a sports medicine professional who is willing to educate and capable of educating you about the role of your mind in the injury process and how to use it most effectively to ensure rapid, complete recovery can be an important step in healing your injury.

As a runner, you know of the role of stress in the onset and continuance of illness and injury. You may justifiably ask, *To what degree can psychological stress hamper performance and make me more injury prone?* And, once injured, *To what extent does stress interfere with and delay my healing process?*

Stress will elevate your heart rate and blood pressure, increase your daily energy requirements, and detract from the quality of your sleep. The combined effects of these variables will decrease your body's ability to heal quickly. Be aware that your view of an upcoming race event could wreak havoc with your body. Situations themselves are not stressful—it is your perception of the circumstances that causes stress. Running hills increases anxiety for some, while others view them as sheer joy. Hills are hills; they don't change. What changes is how you choose to view them—and this will determine how they affect your performance.

Becoming anxious and frightened by your view of "the wall" in a marathon, for example, can raise your stress level to such a point that it could inhibit muscle fluidity, slowing you to a snail's pace. Severe cramping and injury are distinct possibilities. Interpreting the race as a situation for possible disaster can result in various emotional stress reactions. Feelings such as panic, tension, pressure, or anxiety can and often do lead to physiological responses that can inhibit performance. Such a defensive posture makes your body vulnerable to injury.

Once injured, you are subjected to even more stress, which will significantly interfere with the healing process; being injured is itself stressful. This secondary-stress syndrome creates additional panic and fear. Pain is now intensified as the new stress reduces blood circulation to the injured area and keeps the muscle tense; such reactions prolong the recovery process.

Once you understand this mind–body connection with regard to injuries, it becomes much easier for you to try various strategies that facilitate your ability to change perceptions of stressful situations and to work on reducing postinjury tension and anxiety. You become more willing to use your mind as an adjunct to hastening recovery. It is always satisfying to see an athlete perceive the prognosis for the injury as hopeful; anxiety and tension diminish, and healing seems to begin immediately.

Treatment With the Mind

The following mind-sets will help to facilitate the healing process and contribute to rapid and complete recovery. Effective therapies such as medical, chiropractic, and massage may also be indicated. Regardless of the physical treatment you choose, do not neglect the psychological issues and the power of a positive mind-set to facilitate the healing of injury.

Crisis Is Opportunity

A running injury is very much a crisis for each of us. But just as we learned to view failure as an opportunity for learning, we can also view an injury as an opportunity. A track coach at a major Division I university stated that his cross-country team consistently ran fatigued with poor performances. He would not have anything to do with reducing their workload, and by midseason three of the top four runners became injured. This crisis helped him to realize that changes were in order. He took this opportunity to modify the program, reduce the intensity, and allow the athletes time to rest and taper more drastically before a race. These alterations made a huge impact the following year as the team captured the regional championship, injury free.

Opportunities await you in your crisis as well. Consider your downtime as a chance to catch up on other important aspects of life that may have been neglected because of your rigorous training program. It is also an excellent time to reevaluate priorities and put things in perspective. For example, you could devote more time to your family or work. You could learn more about the training and physiology of running. You could start a yoga or weightlifting class, create a new logbook format, or go enjoy a local high school or college track meet to gain new appreciation for the sport. You could take the opportunity to focus on other aspects of training: hone your visualization and relaxation techniques, or develop a strength training or stretching program. These activities can help you feel as if you are still making progress and improving parts of your running. When you begin to change your view of the crisis, you will begin to mitigate your stress, panic, anxiety, and tension; as a result, you will hasten your healing and come back with greater vitality and enthusiasm.

Panic Reduction

The most prevalent response to running injury or illness is panic; the most essential ingredient for healing and recovery is hope. A doctor told a runner with a severe injury that two out of five athletes never fully recover from this setback. The athlete began to experience panic and increased pain due to this uncertainty. At the suggestions of his coach, he went to another physician whose office staff was upbeat and positive. When he told the doctor about the two of five statistic, she quickly replied, "Yes, but three out of five do just fine, and I'll do what I can to help you be one of those three." Filled with hope and optimism, he followed the doctor's program, recovered completely, and is back to racing full time. Cautious optimism infuses hope. Why stoke the fires of panic? This will not aid your recovery.

Mood Shifters

It is extremely difficult to exist each day without the emotional high from your workouts that you rely on. It has been shown that runners who suddenly stop exercising experience mood shifts and altered levels of neurotransmitters in the brain that can bring on depression. To counteract these effects, try pool running or stationary bike riding. Such cross-training gives you that good feeling psychologically and also stimulates the flow of blood to the injured area, quickening the healing process. Because of this experience, you may realize the value of cross-training when you resume your running program to help the body to sustain itself— injury free—for many years to come.

Laughter Medicine

Grandma was right, her beliefs being validated by modern scientific studies: laughter is the best medicine. Humor is an important asset when coping with injury. Research supports the notion that positive emotions, stimulated by laughter, cause the brain to secrete endorphins—endogenous opiates—that relieve pain and tension.

Try viewing outrageous comedy videos, and notice how your pain subsides. It is important to recognize that we tend to take our sport and ourselves too seriously. Notice how much better you feel when you lighten up a bit and realize that your injury is probably not life threatening, but a temporary inconvenience that will eventually heal.

Seeing and Healing

The national teams of Russia, Germany, and other Eastern European countries have effectively used visualization and imagery for the healing of athletic injury. We have had great success with many of our client runners using this technique in conjunction with other treatment modalities to help with healing and to better cope mentally.

Doctors and researchers are now demonstrating and documenting the incredible benefits of visualization in treatment programs for athletes with serious injuries. They notice that images are so powerful, they can seemingly prod the immunological system into destroying even the greatest malignancy. They show a high correlation between positive results and positive attitudes in patients who use mental imagery in concert with other traditional therapeutic approaches.

Visualization is a good technique for coping mentally when injured because it reduces fears and anxieties athletes experience when injured. These emotions create vasoconstriction, which restricts blood circulation to the injured area and delays healing. By eliminating those destructive emotions, relaxation and visualization allow normal blood flow to resume and facilitate the mending process. Relaxation allows the body to function optimally by decreasing stress; visualization sends powerful messages to the brain to stimulate the body in its healing and helps to reduce the pain. Visualization gives you the feeling that you're in charge by requiring you to take control of the recovery process (see visualization exercises at the end of this chapter).

Reflect and Genuflect

Take the time to reflect and be thankful for what you do have. What if this situation came to you for a reason? Rather than ask, *Why does this hurt so much?* or *Why me?* ask yourself, *What is this pain telling me? Why is it here at this time?* Take some time and keep coming back to these deeper questions. Listen to the responses. Focus on your life and put your running in perspective with everything else. In a recent interview with world-champion cyclist Lance Armstrong about his battle with cancer, he candidly said, "You know, the house, the car, the money, the fame . . . I'd give it all away in a second to be cancer free. It all really doesn't mean anything unless you have your health." Sometimes we don't realize this until we have our health taken away. Perhaps the injury is a blessing in disguise; accept it as such. Yield and bow to it, rather than fight it. Remember, if you resist, it will persist.

Visualization

In a deeply relaxed state with eyes closed, visualize the following to help you in the healing of your injury or illness.

Visualize the place of injury or illness.

See armies of white blood cells rushing to the infected or injured area.

Picture the color of the illness or injury (usually a deep red).

See hundreds of people massaging the area with a healing ointment.

Feel it penetrate deeply into the area.

Picture the color changing (pinkish in tone).

See the bone or tissue knitting together, or the illness gone.

Imagine being totally healed, stronger and better than before.

Affirmations

Use the following affirmations with your visualization, create your own, and recite them each day for maximum health and healing.

Every day in every way, I get stronger and healthier.

I always strive to be injury free.

Recovering my health is a big part of myself.

I use my injury (or illness) as a helpful wakeup call.

I am an injury-free, vibrant runner.

_____

_____

_____

_____

chapter 15

Reversing
the Aging Process

Satchel Paige once said, "Age is mind over matter; if you don't mind, it won't matter." While running at 9,000 feet in the mountains east of Los Angeles, I (Jerry) met three athletes who didn't seem to mind. I was lost, and stopped to ask for directions. Impressed by their knowledge of the backcountry, I inquired as to how often they came to this area. One of the gentlemen claimed that he's been exercising in these hills five days a week since he started running seven years ago—on his 70th birthday. You don't need to be a rocket scientist to figure out that he's 77 years of age. His two buddies were 78 and 74.

We can't begin to tell you how inspired we are by the attitudes and physical conditioning of these three amigos, poignant reminders about what lies ahead for us as we run with the deer in the mountains, running up and down beautiful trails for perhaps another 30 or 40 years. We feel overjoyed at the prospect of such adventure. Exercise physiologists have shown that a fit 70-year-old can have the same aerobic fitness as a sedentary 25-year-old. Therefore, they can both expect to be able to carry out similar physical challenges. Further, research has shown that seniors who train vigorously can slow down the rate of decline aging tends to have on the body. Both men and women have shown remarkable fitness levels as 70- to 80-year-olds.

On a similar note, we were both invited to give a few presentations to groups of sports doctors, professionals, and athletes prior to the Hawaiian Ironman competition. While there, we received an invitation to attend a special party for—as we were told—an unusual group of athletes. We were astounded to find out that the celebration was in honor of 14 men and women who would compete the next day in the grueling 2.4-mile swim, 112-mile bike ride, and 26.2-mile run. All of these athletes were in their 70s.

Stories like these give us a boost and teach us that aging need not be the obstacle to fitness it is often thought to be. People all over the world are beginning to redefine the aging process and act as models who encourage and instill within each of us the notion that we can perform well into our 70s, 80s, and beyond.

Although aging does have an effect upon performance and there are some real physiological limitations that should be considered, how they influence you personally depends on your approach to fitness, both physically and mentally. The effects of aging on exercise performance can vary significantly from one individual to the next.

One thing is certain: the data that have been collected over the years on running and fitness with aging is limited to a sample of people who are mostly sedentary. (The above examples are unusual and basically unaccounted for.) Decline in such a group will be quite different from that of a whole new generation of active baby boomers who, turning 50 at the rate of one every seven seconds, are likely to carry their vitality and fitness programs for many years to come. This will significantly improve the findings about the population of people who are basically sedentary.

Change Happens

There is no doubt about it—the body becomes less efficient as we age. For one, aerobic capacity ($\dot{V}O_2$max), an important component of all endurance sports, begins to decline as we age. There is less blood flow to the muscles, meaning less oxygen and a subsequent drop in energy. Your muscular system loses the mass it once had, along with some elasticity and mobility. Aerobic potential, the ability of the body to break down carbohydrates with oxygen, declines. As a result, it becomes difficult to handle strong efforts such as running hills, sprinting, or any other all-out activity. Hard workouts that once required only a day or two of recovery take three or more days to come back from as we age. And, with respect to speed, it has been estimated that the average runner experiences a decrease of 5 percent per decade.

Reversing the Norm

Even though the data collected from studies on aging and performance indicate an inevitable decline as we get older, the question arises: are the findings valid, and if so, are they reliable? The answer to both may be yes—for the subjects used. But are they an accurate representation of what is possible? After all, how well trained was the sample? Did they live a wellness lifestyle? What was the quality of their workouts? How much? How intense?

How is it that an athlete can continue to run well beyond where most have stopped? It appears that the use or disuse of the body controls the rate of most physiological deterioration. New findings point to the notion that going up in years doesn't necessarily mean going down in vitality. Researcher and runner Ken Cooper claims that decline with age in not inevitable. The three amigos and triathletes we opened this chapter with testify to this. And then there are stories about runners such as Hal Higdon, who, in his 50s, ran a marathon under 2:30; John Kelley, well into his 70s, had the physical conditioning of a fit 40-year-old. Ruth Wysocki is continuing to run well in her 40s among American women distance runners. We now have elite runners like Frank Shorter and Bill Rodgers who will probably shatter most myths we have about aging and performance as they race into their 50s and beyond.

According to author, endurance athlete, and coach Joe Friel, intensity and volume may be the most important variables in the aging performance equation. Having written much on aging and performance, he talks about many athletes who have maintained excellent aerobic function into their later years by keeping intensity and volume high. Research in this area demonstrates quite well that when an athlete maintains high training intensity and volume, fitness levels can even improve. Friel concludes that the slowing down that occurs after age 50 is not due to age, but to self-imposed limitations on training—which can be reversed. He says that half the loss is due to inactivity, and another fourth results from reduced intensity. It appears that disuse is the major culprit with performance and aging. Advancing years may only be responsible for a quarter of the physiological losses, a total of 2.5 percent every 10 years.

So to reverse any possible decline in performance with aging, or even to maintain your high level of fitness, realize that vigorous, high-intensity, frequent workouts will help you to stay fit. In this way, heart stroke volume remains high, blood vessels stay open and flexible, and your lungs will continue to function more efficiently. Friel recommends a program that combines high-intensity training (hills and intervals), weight training, stretching, good nutrition, rest, and consistent mental exercise (using the concepts in this book) to counteract the downside of aging. It should also be pointed out, however, that the recovery needs of older athletes often are greater. You need to listen to your body and give it more rest between these intense workouts if needed.

Run Longer, Run Wider

For years, many believed that running had little effect on lengthening one's life. With the untimely death of the famous author and runner Jim Fixx, some even suggested that such exercise could kill you. The truth is, Fixx had a diseased heart because of his many prerunning years of smoking and an unhealthy lifestyle (not to mention any genetic predisposition to heart disease he might have had). Running probably extended his life for 12 or more years.

Numerous studies now are indicating that running's impact on the overall health and well-being of those who work out can contribute to longevity. For example, runners rarely smoke, are usually not overweight or are maintaining a consistent weight, eat healthy diets, have more efficient cardiovascular and pulmonary systems, are more relaxed and less depressed, and feel a sense of self-worth—all the right stuff to defend against the leading causes of death in the United States, heart disease and cancer. Runners, therefore, likely do live longer. Even if you believe that runners do not live longer, they probably live wider than they otherwise would by being healthier day to day.

To help you keep this vigorous lifestyle going for this decade and more to come, we recommend that you walk these 10 steps on the stairway to a long, vibrant, energetic, happy running life for as long as you live. Here are the 10 R approaches to aging well.

Run often. Consistent exercise is crucial. It's better to run 5 miles each day than to do 15 miles twice a week. Your body will stay adjusted to the everyday movement and not fall asleep after three or four days of nothing. Remember, it's good to wear out your running shoes; it means you must be in shape.

Ride occasionally. Take a break from your runs and climb on a bike. The change will keep your passion for running fresh, and you'll enjoy the territory you'll be able to cover on wheels. A good 25-mile ride gives you the equivalent of a strong 10-mile run. Nothing is lost . . . much is gained.

Race frequently. This step helps you to set goals that challenge you and provides you with the intensity factor that we talked about earlier in the chapter. Vigorous workouts are easier with a group, and racing provides this naturally.

Rely on others. Join a group or a club. Have a running buddy.

When you rely on others, they rely on you. Knowing that you're expected to be at the park at 7 A.M. to join the group will keep you on track. The social benefits as a result of this are numerous and contribute to your overall lifestyle of fun and wellness.

Relax. Be sure to take the time each day you train to meditate, visualize, and use your affirmations prior to your workout. Taking time to rest and relax recharges the body and soul. You will notice how your energy, lost throughout the day, will begin to return when you take time out to recover. This becomes even more important as you age.

Reps of weight training. Don't forget to include a weight training program with your running. As we age, we run the risk of losing large amounts of muscle mass unless we continue to maintain or build by lifting light weights with high repetitions. Talk with someone knowledgeable before you begin, in order to avoid overdoing it or to guard against potential injury.

Relish good foods. Refuse to eat processed substances, which can be toxic to your body. Instead, fill your world-class body with the best nutrition—fresh fruits, vegetables, whole grains, lean meats. Be moderate with alcohol and caffeine. Consider food to be the fuel you ingest to feel good at higher levels of performance. Be sure to hydrate often with water. High fluid intake will help prevent cramping and other problems associated with dehydration.

Read good books and magazines. This is more food for the soul, keeping the mind stimulated and alert. Consider that which opens your heart to your greatest human potential, and in this way you train not only the body and mind, but the spirit as well.

Reflect. When you take time to relax during your day, be sure to reflect upon your running journey—where you were when you began and how far you have come, not only as an athlete, but as a person. Feel appreciative and fortunate that you have the gift of running. Reflect upon the periodic cycles and fluctuations in performance; what can be gained from contemplating these natural ups and downs?

Rest Your Body. Remember to stress, then rest. This is even more crucial as we age. Your interval training should be followed by a pause, during which you run a moderate or easy workout or take a complete day off. Rest is the single most important ingredient in the recipe for successful running into the advancing years.

The bottom line on aging and running performance is this: we do not know our limits. The real barrier seems to be the mind, not the body. According to most experts, our true life span is 100-plus years, and whether we make it has much to do with our attitudes, beliefs, and lifestyles. Our bodies are simply waiting for our minds to give them permission to go beyond what most of us think is the finish line.

Visualization

In a deeply relaxed state with eyes closed, visualize the following to help you challenge the myths about aging and performance:

Imagine yourself running in a race.

Feel strong and fluid.

Hear a competitor come up on your shoulder and pass you.

Notice that this runner appears to be 10 to 15 years younger.

Notice how fit and smooth the runner is as she begins to pull away.

Imagine staying with her, catching up and surging on by, and finishing the race in front of her. After the race, imagine talking with this person and finding out there's a 20-year age difference.

Feel excited and inspired by your superb performance and how this person motivated you to run beyond belief.

Affirmations

Recite the following, and visualize them as well. Create a few of your own:

Age is mind over matter.

I refuse to give age permission to limit my horizons.

I continue to run well now and into the future years.

I run with great vigor and intensity.

_____

_____

_____

_____

V

Running Beyond

Today, thousands of runners are discovering that their sport is a physical avenue to obtaining something much wider and deeper. We are talking about a harmony between body, mind, and spirit, where running becomes the means to experience a personal potential greater than one's physical self. It is a state of going beyond by pushing against our psychobiological limits and beliefs, and it has been experienced by runners long before the so-called running boom. Well over 300 years ago, Native American warriors would cover hundreds of miles at a time and experience the wide-open spaces of their minds.

In this final part of the journey, we will help you to add a new dimension to your running. In chapter 16, you will become inward bound and discover your personal rhythms as you run to your own inner beat for a more satisfying level of participation, a level called mastery. You will begin in chapter 17 to experience the mystical connection between your running exertion and the subsequent changes within the mind. Finally, in chapter 18 you will discover that running is indeed a heavenly dance between you and your sport, one in which you give yourself over to your natural movement, and put all aside for that sacred hour, to just play and dance the dance.

chapter 16

Training for Mastery

We have given much thought to the notion of mastery. To be a master is to be the epitome of perfection. Right? Wrong. Nothing could be farther from the truth. A master is a master because he recognizes the fact that he is always only halfway there. Mastery is a journey of never-ending multidimensional movement, every stage being our teacher and mentor, guiding us on a zigzag path toward excellence. There is no definitive end, just a flowing into a space that is bigger, wider, and deeper than where we began.

For the purpose of this journey, we differentiate between joggers, runners, and masters. A jogger moves with the feet; a runner runs with the feet and mind; the master glides effortlessly with her feet, mind, and spirit all working together simultaneously. Mastery is not something to be ultimately attained; it is simply a process or journey available to all joggers and runners who are willing to walk (or run) the path and never get off.

The path of mastery is not a smooth one, and many factors in your world can (and do) sabotage your efforts to stay on track. Impatience and a lack of perseverance complicate this journey. We are not very good at delayed gratification—we want instant mastery. This, according to the spirit of mastery, is a contradiction in terms. Mastery is the commitment to a lifestyle of excellence, not a destination at which you arrive. Running within is the masterful journey; mastery is important because it facilitates your ability to become your best and experience much joy in the process. The steps to relax, visualize, and affirm your experience as a runner as well as all of the other precepts throughout this book can help to move your running lifestyle toward mastery and excellence.

Metaphorically, mastery is a river. It changes direction and, at times, seems to go back to where it started. The pace quickens rapidly through the narrows, yet dramatically slows as the river widens. Sometimes the water is clear; sometimes murky and cloudy, exhilarating yet placid, raging yet calm. If you try to slow it down, you struggle; if you speed up when it slows down, it will resist. You can't push the river. The most exuberant journey is to give yourself over to its power. If you could see the river's path (your mastery journey) from a higher perspective, you would see clearly that there is a beginning and a definite direction, a natural progression and flow. And like the river, mastery has its ups and downs, turns and surprises. You need to trust the experience—

especially when forward progress levels out or plateaus—that you will continue to make the gains toward the larger body of water, the sea, the arena of unlimited potential.

Diligent Preparation

On the journey of mastery, preparation or practice is the reward. The slow movement along the path requires you to practice your running diligently. You live for the training runs. You begin to enjoy your workouts not just for the workouts, but for the whole experience of running—how it makes you feel physiologically, emotionally, and spiritually. This is the real treasure, and the medals, trophies, and accolades at the end of the race are simply the by-products of this experience. The true prize is the practice, the in-the-moment warrior runner experience.

The mastery growth curve is a long, gradual climb. As we've noted in previous chapters, it takes most of us 5 to 7 years of practice until our bodies begin to take form. In fact, physiologically most runners can continuously improve for 10 years from the time they start running, regardless of how old they are when they begin. All that is required is a pair of legs, a properly applied progressive training program, and a will to be a better runner.

Mastery—a high level of proficient, competent, versatile wizardry—is available to all who enter the running arena, regardless of past experiences. Your inability to rise to a lifestyle of running excellence in prior times is not reason to prevent you from enjoying high masterful levels of participation through the natural process of noticing your shortcomings and doing what it takes to go beyond them: practice.

Practice, Practice, and More Practice

Mastery is an endless journey that requires one small step at a time. Your success on this journey is measured by the quality of those steps and your attention to the practice. When you want to experience mastery at anything, do not look for a quick fix; there are no immediate results.

The Chinese symbols for practice first show a young bird flapping its wings, then depict the bird in flight once it feels confident enough to fly. When you wish to learn how to do your "flying" on the way to ultimate running, remember the metaphor of the bird. You must constantly repeat your practicing of a certain skill until your spirit takes flight, soaring with joy and enormous magnitude. And no matter how good you get at your game, there's always the need for repetition with variation if you want to keep flying.

One visible world-class athlete who seems to have no trouble flying and soaring is Michael "Air" Jordan. Michael keeps aloft of his competitors because he insists on practicing continuously. He has been known to show up early on game day and, in the absence of his teammates, work on his three-point shot over and over until he nears perfection. If an athlete as great as Jordan understands the need to practice repeatedly, perhaps all of us runners should consider its value in our physical endeavors, just as John Wooden, coach of the powerful UCLA Bruins basketball dynasty, understands: "The road to mastery is through the eight laws of learning: explanation, demonstration, imitation, repetition, repetition, repetition, repetition, and repetition."

Physiologically speaking, neurological pathways between the brain and muscles are recruited and synchronized with repetitious training. Each individual muscle fiber, through training, becomes more efficient and thereby produces more power more quickly. In the brain, the exercise behavior has "learned" to become more automatic and less stressful as we adapt to the training load.

Plateau: The State of Continual Learning

When you practice your running, you begin to notice steady, subtle, continual progress that is quite satisfying. Gains are inevitable with daily attention to learning any skill or technique. Progress is possible as long as the training loads are sufficient to shock the athlete into a period of new growth and adaptation. It does take time and diligent work, and unfortunately, the more closely you approach your physical potential, the more challenging it becomes to shock your body without simultaneously causing an injury. Thus, there will be the plateaus along the way—

periods of relative stability when there is a little or no apparent progress or benefit. See this absence of progress as another important, necessary aspect of the upward learning curve. The plateau can be used as a natural pause—an important time of reflection, reevaluation, revelation, and perhaps rest, part of the periodic cycle where you level out before you spurt ahead. It is a sacred time, offering you the chance to work with your feelings of frustration and annoyance.

If preparation is the prize, the plateau is the professor, the teacher, the place where learning is continual, even if unnoticeable, and you seem to be getting nowhere. You must be willing to hang out and do most of your running on a plateau until your body's innate intelligence absorbs all that's new, all the unfamiliar movement and exertion. According to martial artist and author George Leonard, we need to love the plateau and enjoy the fruits of our accomplishments, as we get ready to surge again only to accept the new plateau that invariably awaits all of us. As a runner, begin to love those level-out periods of learning.

To help yourself with the plateau, don't fight it or push it aside. See it for what it is—an essential step for anyone who chooses to be on the road of excellence. Finally, be kind to yourself, like a good self-coach, and remember that breakthroughs are waiting in the wings. Physiologically, ask yourself, *How do I feel today?* Keep the answers to this recurring question in your logbook, along with your other mind–body input. Rate your sleep quality, appetite, and mood. Pay close attention to your perceived exertion and muscle soreness during your workouts. How do your legs feel walking up stairs? Record your morning resting heart rate. Reflect on your training and decide whether your plateau is a result of overtraining or undertraining. If the answer is not obvious, then reduce training by 50 percent for several weeks and see how your body responds. Here is your opportunity to experience how a calm and adaptable demeanor along with good-natured persistence will help you through this trying time on the journey of mastery.

Go Slower, Arrive Sooner

We encourage all athletes not to rush the process of becoming their best; to know that mastery takes time. Go slower, arrive sooner is the ultimate paradox of athletic accomplishment. Ancient wisdom encourages a calm observation of the natural unfolding of events. Rapid growth and advancement are unnatural. Therefore, it is wise to avoid haste and enjoy the journey as you evolve into the ultimate runner. Know that all things occur at the appropriate time. Patience is the ability to enjoy and immerse yourself in the process, the flow of your running, as it assumes its own form and shape.

A runner went to her coach and asked how long it would take to develop into a world-class athlete. He reassured her that if she trained properly, it would take four to five years to fully develop. Feeling frustrated and uneasy about this, she told him she didn't want to wait that long. In an attempt to force the issue and arrive on the scene sooner, she asked how long it would take if she worked harder, faster, and with more effort. Ten to twelve years was his reply. As sports medicine clinicians, we have seen this many times—runners overtrain and become subject to overuse injuries as a result of thinking that more training is better and will help one meet goals more rapidly. The problems can manifest as either a series of recurring overuse injuries or chronic fatigue syndrome, affecting the entire system. The bottom line is that with chronic injuries due to overtraining, you will never achieve sufficient training loads to produce prolonged improvement.

Therefore, the journey of mastery asks that you enter into a new time zone in which you slow down to go faster. Running creates numerous opportunities for you to slow down, develop, and practice the virtue of patience. We recommend that you develop strength in this area through *wait training:* notice the natural flow of events and then act accordingly. This requires constant vigilance as you monitor your progress with regard to levels of energy, fatigue, soreness, staleness, slumps, plateaus, spurts, enthusiasm, and burnout. Too much, too soon, that familiar hurry-up sickness, invariably leads to injury or illness—nature's way of telling you to slow down, reevaluate, and take a break. Learn to read your body, and initiate small adjustments in your training to avoid excess overload and injury.

Don't think of mastery as the capacity to endure, or as an act of perseverance. See it, instead, as the willingness to be at peace and give yourself time to develop as an athlete without placing limits on how long it will take to reach mastery. Mastery is a mind-set that goes beyond the connotation of suffering. This is not about pain in any way. Remember that all things occur not when we think they should, but when the time is right. There is a natural flow, like the river, with the path of mastery; chaos results when you try to hasten this natural process.

Think for a moment about the race between the tortoise and the hare. Through the inner qualities of consistent, deliberate, steady, slow movement, the tortoise arrived sooner than the quicker yet more spastic, inconsistent, and fatigued hare. Haste does, indeed, make waste. And remember, if your running life is a good one, a life of mastery, most of it will be spent on a plateau.

Visualization

In a relaxed state with eyes closed, visualize the following in order to help yourself accept the plateau on your mastery journey:

See yourself during a running training session.

Imagine repeating a certain routine over and over until it feels monotonous.

Shift your consciousness and discover the joy and worth of the repetitious moment, knowing that your body is learning and improving.

Feel yourself enjoying the plateau, a place to reflect on your past and future potential, a place to accumulate knowledge for your next spurt.

Tell yourself that breakthroughs are waiting to happen.

See yourself performing a week later as you achieve the breakthrough you've wanted.

Affirmations

Use the following with your visualization, create new ones of your own, and recite them all each day.

All things come my way when I practice every day.

I enjoy the way of mastery more than mastery itself.

Practice is a joy, my eternal delight.

My patience is the virtue of my success.

_____

_____

_____

_____

chapter 17

Experiencing the Mystical

Sister Marion Irvine, a Catholic nun, once said that she never felt more connected to her Creator than she did while running through the best natural environments. To her, this was the ultimate mystical experience—a state of going beyond the ordinary, a sense of unity with all that surrounds you, a moment in time when everything seems to fall into place. Amazingly, Sister Marion held onto this view, and in her 50s ran fast enough to qualify to run the 1984 Olympic Trials marathon.

We are far enough along the path of mastering the body–mind–spirit connection to consider the idea of going beyond our psychobiological limits, the emergence of hidden reserves and capacities, to witness the mystical connection between our physical activity and extraordinary transformations of the mind. It is now time to touch base with your runner spirit and notice how you have added new dimension to your sport and become more aware of running within. You are now ready to experience magical encounters that can happen when you run—in the mountains or on hills and trails; with the deer, eagles, and other creatures—and recapture the innocence, the momentary bliss, the passionate connection to the deeper reasons to run. Here is the mystical going beyond, that which you thought impossible, times where you seem to run out of your body and into another dimension.

Going Beyond

Jon Sinclair is one of the most impressive elite distance runners. He is well aware of going beyond. "I've given it much thought," Sinclair states when asked if he's experienced extensional peak moments. "I've had several occasions when everything clicked and I was running in what seemed to be greased grooves." He attributes it to "proper communication with my body." Jon also refers to this feeling as "gliding effortlessly" across the road. As you watch him "glide" on the beautiful tartan track at the Olympic Training Center, you can't help but think of how his stride is like a hydroplane, swiftly flowing above the surface. Poetry in motion. His movement mimics the weightlessness experienced only by astronauts floating in a space capsule, defying all the laws of gravity. According to Sinclair, the feeling is one of "gliding without putting any energy into maintaining momentum." He is quick to point out that speed, rather than being the root of pain, is a source of ecstasy that many runners overlook or misunderstand. Athletes for years have referred to ecstasy as the love of a struggle. The struggle and the energy release from a good speed workout may very well prove ecstatic. Of his most difficult, struggling workouts, Sinclair states that "they are the worst feelings in the world . . . and the best."

A state of going beyond should not be confused with the release of beta endorphins commonly experienced after a grueling workout; that's a runner's high. Peak experiences, although they may involve a release of such natural opiates from the brain, have a much broader scope. In their book *The Psychic Side of Sports,* Michael Murphy and Rhea White make it clear that when we push against our psychobiological limits, the brain tissues record a remarkable range of mystical pleasures: extraordinary inner vision, peace, stillness, calm, detachment, freedom, floating, ecstasy, power, control, immortality, unity, mystery, and awe. These are but a few of the psychic rewards of sport, otherwise known as the peak experience.

Examples of mystical experiences and journeys can be found in Peter Nabokov's *Indian Running,* where he offers a glimpse into the world of Native American ritual. These runners would often anticipate life-directing visions that would come to them on these dream-like sojourns. They seemed to run with boundless energy, running easily for 170 miles without stopping.

Many runners tell us that they hear solutions to problems, answers to questions, and input on decisions to be made while on long, peaceful runs. During these moments, they feel as though they are floating and gliding over the terrain, surrounded by the trees that envelop them, enjoying a feeling of being totally free, as if they could go on forever.

Mystical running is the opportunity to get quiet, center your energy, reflect, meditate, and silence the inner chatter and noise of your busy life to access your creative self. Poets, philosophers, scientists, and naturalists have always known that the best ideas, thoughts, and creations come to us more easily in solitude, on foot and in motion. Thoreau, Plato, Einstein, Wordsworth, and Lao-Tzu sauntered through woods and over the hills to achieve mental clarity, fresh, original thoughts, and epiphanies to help replenish their souls and sustain their imaginations to illuminate their work and all of life.

Experience the Mystical

Spending time alone and in motion will open the floodgates for the incessant flow of your creative juices as it has for other visionaries. New ideas can and will begin to flood your stream of consciousness as you turn inward in this state of solitude, one of the most precious assets of the running life.

If you become silent during your physical activity, you have the chance to experience as you move across the terrain what we call *stillness in motion*, a dreamy, meditative state with brief moments of quietude. Just as a cloudy pond becomes clear when free of agitation, your mind, filled with emotional debris, gains clarity from this period of reverie or stillness within. It is a peaceful state, an inner environment where your suppressed thoughts begin to surface and visions begin to blossom, where a mystical oneness with the beauty of nature takes place.

As the mystical runner, we ask that you actively begin to synchronize the inner, intuitive mind with the moving body. Visualization, used throughout this book, can help in this regard. Combining visualization with movement enables you to become aware of the dynamic growth potential that lies within and beyond the boundaries of competition. Running itself offers a natural chance for short hibernation and quietude, a sense of peace and meditation, an escape from the noise of the electronic age. Like the bear who quietly enters the mountain stream, swimming around and waiting patiently for his dinner to arrive, you can begin to use your runs as opportunities to do some swimming in your own stream of consciousness. Use this meditative time to help you crystallize your thoughts, make decisions, solve problems, and even answer challenging, penetrating questions. Take a step back, get off the treadmill of life, and run alone in quiet, safe environments, allowing the freshness of the day to help you find your own sacred inspiration and personal landscape.

From Sole to Soul

As a mystical runner, let your physical sole open up pathways to your innermost soul, and experience the rapture of being fully alive. During this time when you run, when your world is free of distractions, when your mind is quiet and all comes to a stop, take the opportunity to focus on what's important to you, and decide, if necessary, what you wish to do about it. It is here that you have the chance to discover the answers to life's most important spiritual questions: *Who am I? Where am I going? With whom?* And finally, the ultimate unanswered question: *What's it all about?* The answers will come from the depths of your running soul.

Digging deeply from sole to soul, Olympian marathoner Bob Kempanian discovered what it was all about during his experience while winning the 1996 Men's Olympic Trials. You must know who you are and where you are going in order to endure such a test of the spirit. Bob was running a 5-minute-per-mile pace, comfortably in the lead and in control, when with several miles to go, he started to vomit repeatedly. Essentially, he never broke stride, never really let the vomiting get in his way or foil his plans; he just kept on running. Vomiting is a powerful reflex involving brain stem and limbic functions. However, Bob Kempanian's championlike form was supreme as he stayed focused and maintained cortical control in spite of this distraction. Many athletes would have dropped out of the race, giving up under these circumstances. Bob's response to such an obstacle was to take his performance to a higher plane, one of the mystical runner.

It has been said that the famous Austrian composer Wolfgang Amadeus Mozart was capable of hearing complex musical arrangements in his mind. Much of his brilliant music was written in a relaxed, meditative state. If running is the relaxed, meditative activity that people claim it to be, is it any wonder that some of us experience soulful melodies, rhythms, and other forms of inner sound? Mick Jagger of the Rolling Stones said that he runs up to 5 miles a day prior to an extended concert tour. He claims that it helps him to get in shape physically and spiritually for what lies ahead. I wonder how many of his musical arrangements have come into focus during such exercise? We know of a local Santa

Cruz musician-runner who claims that some of his best songs were conceived on the trails as he ran through the mystical redwoods. This book was partially written after insights gained while we were mountain biking on some of the same trails.

You Can Take a Mystical Journey

Perhaps you haven't experienced such psychobiological phenomena; maybe you have, but failed to make the connection or have forgotten about it. One thing is certain—similar experiences are within reach. You don't need to have the physical abilities of the elite; a strong effort in a regular training run will do it. Understand that such experiences don't happen often; but when they do, you'll now be more aware of them.

As we talk to runners, we are beginning to get the feeling that many of us lose perspective as to why we are putting in the miles. Focusing on faster times and winning is fun, but to do this exclusively is to miss much of what running can offer. The purpose of this journey is to encourage you to go beyond and reach within to experience the many rewards and pleasures of running within. You need to stick with it when your running seems to be going nowhere.

You are now ready to take your own mystical journey, the ultimate running experience. Enter into your run with renewed enthusiasm, with a change of mind and heart, as you celebrate the true meaning of movement as pure play. Discover what awaits you when you become free of analysis, judgment, criticism, and perfection.

Dive into the safe, secure place of noninterference of past attitudes and behaviors. It is the playful path of least resistance as you become totally natural and arrive at a place where you experience your run without any effort. Go for it! Just do it! Feel empowered; you have within you all that you need to experience the mystical aspects of running. Have fun and know that there really is no other purpose to this run than to sustain and enjoy your sport in an effortless fashion and become more personally awakened to enjoy what we call in the next and final chapter on the journey the dance of body, mind, and spirit, the magical dance of the run.

Visualization

In your relaxed state with eyes closed, visualize the following to help you stay connected to your mystical runner.

Picture a peaceful setting, one that you enjoy running in.

Feel yourself glide effortlessly over the terrain.

Sense how relaxed and fluid you are, free of mundane realities.

Hear the birds and the wind filtering through the leaves and branches.

Feel the dreamy meditative state, a moment of solitude.

Notice how you feel at one with nature.

Ask yourself a question that needs to be answered, and wait for an answer.

Hear the answer come to you. If it doesn't, just enjoy the run and try again.

Notice how good it feels to run this way, as if you could go on forever.

Affirmations

Use these with your visualization, create some of your own, and recite each of them daily.

Running offers me a wide range of mystical experiences.

I am open and ready to experience my full creative self on the run.

Running helps me to focus on what's truly important.

_____

_____

_____

_____

chapter 18

Dancing the Dance

When we first begin to run, we tend to approach our running mechanically, overemphasizing the physical—how fast, how far, how much, how often. External concerns such as what we deem to be our ideal weight, outcomes of a race, awards, and recognition seem to be of paramount importance. Indeed, the external aspects of running are important, yet we often overlook the ultimate experience of becoming the dancing runner—one of the greatest gifts running has to offer. In this sense, dance is defined as the coming together of body, mind, and spirit for the purposes of experiencing the joy of the moment and blending with your environment such that you bring out the best in yourself.

Basically, you are the choreographer, the dancer, and the music all rolled into one. With this mind-set, your races become so much more than a competitive opportunity. The race ultimately becomes the excuse to dance with the terrain; with nature; with your buddy; with your physical, mental, and spiritual self. Take for example the Leadville, Colorado, 100-mile endurance race, one of the most difficult races in the world. In addition to the long distance and the hilly trails, the elevation ascends to 12,600 feet above sea level. In 1995, Victoriano Churro Sierra, a 55-year-old Tarahumara Indian from Mexico, came to the race to demonstrate his ability to enjoy the dance. Immediately prior to the race, he fashioned some running shoes out of a car tire and straps of leather. Only someone of passion with deep love for running could do this. As the race wore on, Sierra ran stronger and stronger, eventually taking first place in his imperfect, consistent, deliberate, steady, passionate journey of body, mind, and spirit.

The dancing runner finds more fulfillment when viewing running as passion and bliss. Running often becomes meaningless when your intention is only to conquer the miles, the mountain, the track with your body, simply to achieve fast times and long distances. This may work in the short term, but in the long run it gets tiring and unidimensional.

When most of us begin a running program, we rarely understand the infinite aspects of why we do what we do. Many of us are so preoccupied with the outcomes, results, and technical aspects of our running that we overlook the passion and fun—the reason why we run—rushing instead to reach a goal, as if that were the only purpose of participating. Goals do motivate and keep the drive going initially—yet you can strive to see the bigger picture while still recognizing the purpose of your goals as beacons or stepping stones to meet your challenges, and find greater fulfillment. When you begin to enjoy the dance, you widen and expand your focus and create a bridge to link your body, mind, and spirit so that running can touch every aspect of your being.

Much of the initial resistance many of us may feel toward running has to do with the pressures and tensions related to pushing for outcomes and results. When you feel pressure, know that the key to maintaining your interest and motivation is to come back to the essence of the experience itself, to be in the moment and enjoy the beauty of the activity. You can do this by asking the question *Why am I doing this . . . really?* Get in touch with your inner, deeper motives for wanting to run. You'll discover that much of it has little to do with the outcome or the product. It is the process, joy, satisfaction, and fun that turns you on.

I (Jerry) remember my first few years of running. I enjoyed my races, and even more so those beautiful early morning summer runs in the hills of Boulder, Colorado, seeing herds of deer, smelling the pine trees, and feeling the radiant sun on my skin. It was then that I broadened my scope to see a strong divine connection between my new sport and me. This is the dance that we refer to, in which you totally give in to the natural environment and the movement of your body. Tune in to your form, pace, stride, and fluid movement. Notice how running elevates your spirits and enlivens your body. When you feel this strong connection, you begin to experience the Zen state of *satori*—the union of body, mind, and spirit.

Such a union enables you to experience the ultimate in running. You begin to feel better and better about yourself and your choice to take the time to celebrate the gift that the running life has to offer. You no longer feel separated from your body; you again become one with the rhythms of nature and somehow feel in sync with them, the way that running was meant to be. With this experience, you encounter for the first time, perhaps, the beauty of being alive and the truth about full-spectrum fitness for the ultimate game of life.

Many people claim that running is boring. There is no way that one could respond to this opinion. One simply must experience the passion, ecstasy, and joy; the carefree lightness; the tranquil calm and vulnerability that such movement and play create. Running up a mountain in a relaxed state creates an opportunity to play like a child without concern about whether you will reach the top or whether it will hurt.

On one occasion, I (Jerry) found myself running after a small herd of deer in a beautiful mountain meadow, when a young buck came to a quick stop and began to come toward me. Initially frightened by this aggressive move, I began to realize it was all in play; this gorgeous animal was inviting me to join the group; and I did, as we floated together up and down the canyons. I was one of them; I was a deer. I became a good dancer, at one with nature, in touch with a greater sense of self, feeling the magic of being in the moment and totally letting go.

Such magical moments are available to all of us. Whether you dance with nature, or with someone you love, or simply with yourself, you will recapture the physical and emotional benefits of playing like a child as you enjoy the process. Such is the essence of this dance—the physical enhances the spirit, and you begin to widen your focus as the global effects of your journey toward running within become apparent.

The key to keeping the fires burning well into the night with running (or any arena of life) is to be sure that you follow your bliss and love what you do. When you focus on the beauty and essence of the run, you will cease to experience the anxiety and pressures normally associated with outcomes and results. You will feel good all over.

Fred Rohé talks about experiencing the run as dance. He says in *The Zen of Running*:

> Joy is only known in this moment—now!
>
> So feel the flow of your dance
>
> And how you are not running
>
> For some future reward;
>
> The real reward is now!

Years of running create a "knowing body." The body has innate intelligence and knows what to do. The mind must simply cooperate with what the body already knows and let it do its thing. The mind, by silencing the critical chatter and negativity, becomes the willing partner in this harmonious dance of body, mind, and spirit.

Visualization

In a relaxed state, eyes closed, visualize the following to practice being the dancing runner.

Imagine yourself running in one of your favorite places.

You are free of all obligations and responsibilities at this time.

Feel connected to your personal rhythm and in sync with nature.

Experience the joy and fun as you dance with your surroundings.

Feel better and better about yourself and your choice to dance the run.

Sense the elevation of your spirit and the exhilaration of your body.

Celebrate the beauty of feeling alive.

Affirmations

Use these during your visualization, create some of your own in the blanks, and recite all of them daily.

Focus on the movement, on the flow; dance on, dancing runner.

Now is the moment, enjoy my run.

I am the dancer and the dance.

I look for ways to be completely absorbed in the details of my run.

_____

_____

_____

_____

Bonding With Kindred Spirits

Runners are an unusual collection of moving beings. A man said that he ran from New York to Chicago, nonstop. This is impressive, even if he did do this running in place at the back of the cabin on a plane. He just had to do his long Sunday morning run, and thought that this would do it. He may have been right. In any event, you have to love the eccentricity of it all.

In our professions of sports science, we are fortunate to work with some of the best professional teams and athletes in basketball (NBA), football (NFL), golf (PGA), and cycling. Then there are the numerous collegiate (NCAA) national champions, winter and summer Olympians, and even athletes of the more obscure sports such as skydiving and vaulting (gymnastics on horseback). Even though we love our work with these high-level competitors, the runner captures our spirit. We have totaled 50 cumulative years of running between us, conducting prerace clinics and writing for numerous running magazines over the years. Yet our connection goes deeper than mere credentials.

In thinking about running, we begin to understand this strong connection, an inner kindred bond that draws us close to those in perpetual motion. We experience something that most nonrunners do not. Upon meeting a moving being, a fellow runner, there is a strange manic energy that pulsates between us. Looking deep into each other's eyes, perhaps we get the sense of mutual risks taken, of fears vanquished, of fatigue handled, of challenges overcome, of courage exhibited, of self-doubt confronted, of persistence practiced, of miles and miles being run beyond the point where most intelligent species would have stopped. We've experienced dog-tired muscles and all-out exertion as we find ourselves ready to collapse across the finish line into the arms of a complete stranger, yet feel secure and safe with this person with whom we feel a kindred bond. We grin like dope fiends as we experience the influence of our favorite drugs of choice, endorphins and adrenaline, our rewards for expending more energy in one to three hours than most mortals do in one to three months of exercise. We converse in a language that is absolutely impenetrable to outsiders—splits, speed, LSD, the wall, carbos, fartlek—yet it draws us closer together. We are a weird lot and proud to be part of this insane yet exhilarating experience called distance running.

Actually, when others refer to us as crazy, nuts, or out of our minds, we take these words as, perhaps, the highest compliment ever to be bestowed upon us. Although we're endurance athletes, our goal is not primarily to make our lives longer—we simply wish to make them wider. We are, basically, kindred folks on a lively, high-spirited trek without a finish line, where success is measured solely by the quality of each run, the passion and love for our sport each day for as long as we live.

From this point forward, we ask that you continue to travel this infinite journey of running within, using this book as a dependable, reliable companion.

What you should remember about yourself is that you are a seeker; that's why you take this journey for coming into your own. You seek the answers to running's deeper questions and realize how challenging it is to discover your true self. Yet this does not discourage you, because there is a sense of accomplishment in the quest itself. Essentially, it feels good to simply search and occasionally experience the openings, revelations, and epiphanies that are an integral part of this journey. As you make your way along this never-ending path, we encourage you to go beyond what we offer to you in this book. Our dream is that our work together stimulates in you an even broader perspective of running so that you, the student, can now be the mentor helping others to be mindful in similar and more diverse ways.

Let us encourage you to see this book as a guide, not a doctrine. Its purpose has been to point your feet in the right direction. There are many paths and tributaries that lead toward the main road. Create and design a running program that suits your own personal needs. We want you to do this. Experience what it's like to run within in the ultimate race called life.

Index

A

adrenaline 27. *See also* arousal
affiliation 137
affirmations 41-47. *See also* self talk
  constructing and using 44-46
  defined 12, 41, 43
  examples of 13, 45-46
  negative self-talk 40
  positive, effects of 42
  positive self-talk, guidelines 44
  purpose of 47
  winning 84
affirmations for
  accepting plateaus 174
  aging 164
  being more competitive 76
  believing you can 107-108
  the dancing runner 188
  excessiveness, guarding against 144
  fatigue, control over 128
  focusing 117
  healing 156
  personal goals 99
  risk 70
  staying connected 182
  success 60
  victory 84
aging
  and aerobic capacity 159
  intensity and volume 160
  10 R approaches 162-164
  use or disuse 159-160
  visualization and affirmations 164
Allen, Mark 31, 54
alternative training methods 6, 138-141.
   See also cross-training

anger, effects on optimal performance
  72
Armstrong, Lance 155
arousal
  exercises to increase 27
  optimal desired state of 16-17
  prerace 20
  purpose of 27
athlete, multidimensional *xiv*
attitudes
  alternative 49
  competitive 49
attitudinal shifts, courage and failure
  66-67

B

balance, between relaxation and arousal
  16
Bannister, Roger *xiii*, 30
Beamon, Bob *xii*
beginning distance runner workout
  gentle program of walk-run 6
  moderate approach, benefits of 7
beliefs, unnecessary limitations 102
believing you can 102-103
Benoit Samuelson, Joan 11, 20, 148
Bikila, Abebe 20, 57
body-mind-spirit aspects of performance
  xi, xiii
bodywatching, suggestions for 25
boredom, preventing
  becoming affiliated 137
  changing routine or environment 134
  creating pauses 133
  keep routine rewarding 138
  running for fun 133

varying workout 134
brain. *See also* neurophysiology
    brain stem, responsibilities of 17
    cerebral cortex, responsibilities of 17
    limbic system, responsibilities of 17
breath control 27
breathwatching, techniques for 23-24

C

Campbell, Joseph 79
centeredness 57-58
champions, imitating 103-104
code of the warrior
    accepting loss 57-58
    centeredness 57-58
    inner success 59
    simplicity 56-57
    steadiness 55
compete, derivation of 72
competition
    achieving greater heights 73
    healthy 75
    how to be your best 75
    meaning of (true) 74
competitors
    accepting challenges posed by 74
    embracing as partners, experiment 74
compromise, refusing to 59
concentration
    with consistency 116
    defined 112
    with mantra chanting 116
    objective of 112
confidence
    in abilities to run 82-83
    in decisions during race 82
    in running like a winner 82-83
contest, defined 75
control 80-81
Cooper, Ken 160
courage 63, 65-67
Cousins, Norman 150
cross-training 6-7, 141

D

dance (journey)
    bigger picture, seeing 185
    love what you do 187

    run as 187
    satori 185
    visualization and affirmations 188
disconnection from task 111-112
distraction
    as a challenge 95
    changing your interpretation of 114
    exploring and acknowledging 115-116
    external 113
    internal 113
    pain, physical and mental 95

E

effortless effort 83
egocentric behavior 56
elite runners
    accepting failure 63
    as role models of excellence 103-104
Evans, Lee 30
external distraction, focus internally 113
extrinsic winning
    ephemeral 78
    worst results 78

F

facewatching, techniques for 24-25
failure
    in attaining goals 9
    defined 62
    and elite runners 63
    as a gift 70
    learning from 62-63
    permission to 62
    redirecting 64
    steps to regain perspective 65-67
fatigue
    affirmations for 128
    exercise physiology experiments 124
    forced rest 149
    intrigue 122
    and the mind 123
    neurophysiological aspects of 123
    psychological and physiological components of 122
    shaking off 138
    short-term, aspects of 122-127
    strategies for coping with 123-128

fatigue *(continued)*
  visualization for 128
  wu wei (don't force) 123-124
fear
  attitude shifts for overcoming 62
  physiological responses to 62
fight or flight reaction 41
Fixx, Jim 162
focus 82
  dealing with 95-97
  narrowing, sequence for 114-115
  single-minded for excellence 110
focusing, defined 110
focusing attraction
  strengthening 113
focusing-calming procedures 112-117
Ford, Henry 102
Foreman, Keith 102
Friel, Joe 160

G

Galloway, Jeff 141
goals
  about 1-2
  announcing, pros and cons of 13
  as beacons 4, 97
  being realistic 7-9, 94
  combining 9
  in concert with lifestyle 8
  evaluating abilities 7-8
  failure in reaching 9
  guidelines 7-14
  joy 4, 7
  sharing with others 9
  short-term 7-9
  visualizing 12. *See also* visualization
goalsetting
  impatience and stress 10
  improvement through 10
  reestablishing new goals 11
  setbacks and risks 10-11
Gomez, Bruce 177
Groves, Harry 23, 42

H

health benefits 135-137
Henderson, Joe 56
Higdon, Hal 160

humility 56

I

I Ching 146
images, impact on cells 33
impatience 10
improvement, through goalsetting 10
injury
  controlling, recommendations for
    146-147
  emotional reactions to 147
  estimating mind-set and emotional
    needs 150
  forced rest 149
  keeping your focus with 148
  mind-body connection 150-151
  preventing 142
  recovery, examples of 148-149
  stress, role of with 150-51
  treatment for 150-155
  visualization and imagery for 154
inner powers, discovered *xiii*
integrity
  defined 58
  exhibiting 59
  refusing to compromise 55
internal distraction, focus externally 113
internal victories 78
Irvine, Sister Marion 176

J

Jacobs, Regina 31, 80
Jagger, Mick 180
Jansen, Dan 79, 83
Jordan, Michael 170
Joyner-Kersee, Jackie 64

K

Kelley, John 160
Kempanian, Bob 180
Kennedy, Bob 20
killer instinct 72-73
kindred spirits, bonding with 190-191
knowing body 187

L

Lauck, Anne Marie 20
laughter 153-154

Leonard, George 172
letting go, strategies for 82, 96-97
limbic-cortical balance, physiological analysis of 18-19
limbic system
    experiment for mastering control of 18
    injuries cause stress, correlation to 19, 152
    intense stimulation, results of 17-18
    negative emotions, effects of 19
limits
    examining 102, 104-107
    exercises for 105-106
    four step exercise 105-107
    thinking limits xii-xiii
logbook 2, 65, 172
losing it. *See* panic attack

M

mantra chanting 116
mastery
    being kind to yourself 172
    defined 168
    patience 172
    plateau, as a natural pause 171
    practice 169-170
    preparation for 169
    visualization and affirmations 174
    wait training 173
McMullen, Paul 148
meditation with visualization, benefits of 33
mental training program, affirmation with visualization 45
Mills, Billy 20, 49
mind-sets 1
Mirkin, Gabe 78
mistakes, accepting 57
moderate workout 7
moderation 132-133
modesty, code of the warrior 55-56
Moore, Kenny xii
Moses, Edwin 20
motivation 1, 4, 6
Mozart, Wolfgang Amadeus 180
multidimensional athlete xiv
Murphy, Michael, *The Psychic Side of Sports* 177

music manipulation 27
mystical runner
    higher plane of performance 180
    journey, ultimate running experience 181
    peak experiences 177
    stillness in motion 178
    visualization and affirmations 182

N

Nabokov, Peter, *Indian Running* 177
narrowing your attention prior to a race, exercises for 114-115
natural rhythms 141
negative self-talk, physiological aspects of 40
Nenow, Mark 56-57
neurophysiology, basics of 17
90 percent law 21, 142
no pain, no gain 130

O

opponent
    "feeding" competitive spirit 75
    as a gift for realizing potential 75
overtraining 130-144
    avoiding 131
    natural rhythms, cooperating with 141
    physiological signals 131-32
    psychological signals 132
    self-diagnosing, strategies for 143
    starting again 139-140
    stop running 139
    treatment for 132-134
    visualization and affirmations for 144
Owens, Jesse 72-73

P

Paige, Satchel 158
panic attack 20, 21
patience and persistence, rewards of 9-10
performance, aspects of xi-xii
persistence
    committed 58
    proficient runner and 58
perspective, when setbacks occur 69-70
Pigg, Mike 31

positive words, power of 40-41
postrace strategies 98-99
potential
    redefining 38
    for strengthening body-mind-spirit xi
prance or dance 27
prerace
    arousal 20
    routine, rehearsing 91
    strategies 88-89
        guidelines for 90-94
        visualizing workouts 90
psychophysiological needs 88

R

race
    controlling outcome of 80-81
    course, knowledge of 90-91
    not controlling results of 80
    outcome of, detaching yourself from
        95
    preparation 88
    strategies 94-95
    without care 83
racing
    as a journey, benefits of 82
    opportunity for better performance 64
rapid focus 27
Reevley, Chris 110
relaxation
    for maximum performance,
        techniques 20
    methods of 22-26
    negative thoughts, results of 20-21
    personal level of optimal 16
    physiological responses to 22
    results of too much 16
    for running success 20
relaxed running, achieving 21
relaxed stimulation exercises, purpose
    of 26-27
relaxing the senses, exercises for 26
rest and time off, value of viii
risk(s)
    being courageous 69-70
    benefits of taking 67-68
    for creating courage 68
    failure and success 69

kinds 67
and success 69
ritual
    benefits of 92-93
    defined 92
    flexible and adaptive 93-94
    starting and maintaining 93
Rodgers, Bill 16, 57, 160
Rohé, Fred, The Zen of Running 78, 133-
    134, 187
Rono, Henry xii, 20
Rudolph, Wilma 103
running
    beyond self-imposed limits x
    described ix
    enjoying the process 80
    health benefits, list of 136-137
    loss of interest 133-34. See also
        boredom
    performance, aspects of xi-xii
    for personal fulfillment x
    potential redefining 38
    relaxed 21
    for strengthening body-mind-spirit xi
    within, shifting the mind towards 80

S

satori 185
Scott, Dave 54
seek together ix, 127
Seko, Toshihiko 20, 148
self-knowledge 54-55
self-suggestions, creating your own 13
self-talk, negative and positive 40, 42
setbacks, keeping perspective 69
Shorter, Frank viii, 160
short-term goals
    benefits of 7
    to reinforce winner attitude 7
Sierra, Victoriano Churro 184
simplicity, less is more 56-57
simplicity in training program 142
simulation training
    defined 92
    physiological cues 92
    potential problems 92
Sinclair, Jon 176-77
Snell, Peter 20

soft is strong (aikido), applying 21-22, 94
St. Geme, Ceci 31
steadiness, with meditation, visualization and affirmations 55

T

technique for relaxing, Harry Groves 23
tools for achievement 89
training, visual and physical 31
treatment of injury
    affirmations 156
    cross-training 153
    laughter 153
    opportunities for change 152
    panic, reducing 152
    positive mind-set 151
    reflect and genuflect 155
    thinking limits for *xii-xiii*
    visualization and imagery 154-155
Turnbull, Derek 143

V

victory
    internal 78
    needing 79
    as a path without destination 78
    wanting 79
virtues of the warrior. *See* code of the warrior
visualization 30-38
    in changing functions of the body 34
    consistent, daily practice of 35
    defined 31, 33
    for disappointment and risk 35-36
    effect on muscles, exercise 33, 34
    exercises for the mind 36-37
    five senses, role in 33
    with meditation, benefits of 33
    not just for the elite 35
    for optimal running 34
    for personal goals and concerns 99
    the process 8, 9, 33
    relaxation, prior to race or workout 35
visualization for
    accepting plateaus 174

aging 164
being more competitive 76
the dancing runner 188
excessiveness 144
fatigue 128
focusing 117
healing 155-156
personal goals 99
risk 70
staying connected 182
success 60
total relaxation 60
victory 83-84
visualization techniques
    examples of 30
    power of (mental training) 30-31
    purpose of 31
visual thinking 31, 33
    compared 31
    defined 31
visual training with physical training 31

W

Waitz, Grete 20
Wakiihuri, Douglas 52
warrior runner, characteristics of 52-58
White, Rhea, *The Psychic Side of Sports* 177
winning
    attitudes toward 83
    extrinsic 78
    releasing need to 79
Winter, Bud, "90 percent law" 21, 142
Wooden, John 170
wordwatching
    benefits of 25
    choosing positive, active words 25
workout
    alternate 134-135
    beginning 6-7
Wysocki, Ruth 160

Z

Zatopek, Emil 149
Zen of Running, The 78, 133-134, 187

About the Authors

Jerry Lynch, PhD, is director of the TaoSports Center for Human Potential in Santa Cruz, California. A sports psychologist for more than 20 years, he has worked with many Olympic, national, and world champion runners. He himself was a U.S. regional and national champion distance runner.

Lynch has published six books, including the perennial best sellers *Working Out, Working Within* and *Thinking Body, Dancing Mind: Taosports for Extraordinary Performance in Athletics, Business and Life*, which is available in five languages. These books have been used by athletes on the Chicago Bulls, Detroit Pistons, Cleveland Cavaliers, Houston Oilers, and numerous NCAA Championship teams, as well as by athletic programs worldwide. In addition to writing feature articles and contributing to the "Medical & Training Advice" column in *Runner's World*, he conducts and is available for prerace talks and coaching clinics throughout the United States. Lynch resides in Santa Cruz, California, and can be reached at the TaoSports Center by calling 831-466-3031 or e-mailing Jlynch@taosports.com. For more information, visit www.taosports.com.

Warren Scott, MD, founder and chief of the Division of Sports Medicine at Kaiser Permanente Medical Center in Santa Clara, California, has over 14 years of experience in treating a wide variety of sport related ailments. Scott has conducted several research projects related to injury prevention and trauma control, has been a competitive runner since 1969, and has competed in hundreds of races and triathlons. He has not only served as a physician on the Ironman Triathlon Championship medical team but also completed the Hawaiian Ironman Triathlon himself in 1992.

An accomplished writer, Scott has written articles featured in *Runner's World*, *Triathlon*, and *Better Homes and Gardens* and has written the popular column, "Health Watch," in the *San Jose Mercury News*. He has authored numerous chapters in medical textbooks covering emergency and sports medicine and serves on the science advisory boards for *Runner's World* and *Triathlete* Magazine. Scott is a Fellow of the American College of Sports Medicine and currently resides in Aptos, California.

*You'll find
other outstanding
running resources at*

www.HumanKinetics.com

In the U.S. call

1-800-747-4457

Australia.............................. 08 8277 1555
Canada 1-800-465-7301
Europe......................+44 (0) 113 255 5665
New Zealand................... 0064 9 448 1207

HUMAN KINETICS
The Premier Publisher for Sports & Fitness
P.O. Box 5076 • Champaign, IL 61825-5076 USA